Always in Season

Twelve Months of Fresh Recipes from the Farmer's Markets of New England

WRITTEN BY Elise Richer   ILLUSTRATED BY Teresa Lagrange

To my favorite dining companions: My mother, father, and brother, and Mark, Harry, and Archie, with whom I have shared so many meals.

— ELISE RICHER

To my husband Jim, my children, Gracie and Jack, and my mother. Thank you all for encouraging my creativity.

— TERESA LAGRANGE

ISLANDPORT PRESS
P.O. Box 10
Yarmouth, Maine 04096
www.islandportpress.com
books@islandportpress.com

ISBN: 978-1-934031-69-8
Library of Congress Card Number: 2012945246

Contents

A note on saltiness: All the recipes assume the use of kosher salt. If you are using table salt, please halve the quantity of salt indicated.

Introduction

"The most serious charge which can be brought against New England is not Puritanism but February." —NATURALIST JOSEPH WOOD KRUTCH

FEBRUARY IN NEW ENGLAND can be a wonderful time if you love ice skating, sledding, and franks and beans. If you love local produce, it's tougher. In February, the only local fruits and vegetables available are those coming out of storage. The fall harvest, with its fresh greens and crisp apples, is months behind us. Spring, with its tender lettuces and garlic shoots, is just as distant. For the New Englander trolling the aisles of a winter farmer's market, or opening a winter CSA box, the growing cycles can seem discouragingly brief.

Always in Season's goal is to use what we produce, during the season it is produced, in an enjoyable way. It sounds simple. But mainstream cookbooks sorely neglect many of our vegetables. It's not easy to recall the last time a turnip or rutabaga graced the cover of a popular cooking magazine.

This cookbook follows the New England growing season month by month—including those months when nothing grows—and provides uses for whatever items are either being harvested or coming out of storage. The recipes don't assume that all ingredients will be grown or produced locally. There are just too many things New England cannot produce—olive oil, citrus, and black pepper, for starters—which are essential in the kitchen. The idea is to use our own produce whenever possible, but to supplement with items "from away" as needed, to make the dish palatable and interesting.

The timing of the produce, as well as the list of what is available, is biased toward Maine, where I live. In other parts of New England, the calendar may vary. Connecticut, for instance, produces a respectable number of peaches, but the same cannot be said for Maine. Items also ripen at slightly different times of year. New England is big enough and has varied-enough terrain that several weeks can separate the ripening of crops across the region. Also, different years bring different temperatures and weather. One year, tomatoes come fast and early; another, slow and late. So please treat the calendar divisions herein the way Boston drivers treat traffic lights: as rough suggestions, not exact commands.

It may be too much to ask that on a cold day in February, seeing a head of cabbage in your CSA box will cause your heart to skip a beat, as though you'd glimpsed a half-dozen vine-ripened tomatoes. I'll settle for getting a New Englander to contemplate cabbage without envisioning yet another boiled dinner, and to think about beets without seeing them boiled and buttered. Our farmers and soil have a lot to offer all through the year.

September

cucumber

spinach

zucchini

summer squash

eggplant

cauliflower

September

Cauliflower,
Cucumbers,
Eggplant,
Spinach,
Summer Squash

THIS IS A MONTH of beginnings. The school year is starting, and kids clamor for new backpacks and sneakers. Beaches empty, and college towns fill up with young adults. Moving trucks come and go on city streets. For baseball fans, hopefully September delivers the start of a heated pennant race for the Sox.

This month also means the beginning of fall, marked most vividly by shortening days. Technically, the days have been getting shorter since June, but only now does it become clear how much daylight has slipped away. Mornings feel decidedly cooler than those in August. Many New England farms and gardens are getting their first light frost, marking the start of an emphasis on hardier crops.

Yet going to a farmer's market in September gives the impression that summer is in full swing. Days of sunshine and warmth yield an excellent supply of summery vegetables, allowing us to continue to enjoy that carefree season—at least at suppertime.

Pasta with Cauliflower, Tomatoes, and Cream

When cooking with fresh tomatoes, you can peel the tomatoes beforehand, pick the pieces of skin out of the finished dish, or just eat it all. I stick with the last, which is easiest, and I include seeds, too, because the pulp adds flavor.

SERVES **6**

12 oz fusilli or spaghetti

1 Tbsp butter

1 Tbsp olive oil

1 small head or 1/2 large head of cauliflower, trimmed and cut into bite-size pieces

3 cloves garlic, minced or pressed, in a small bowl with a spoonful of water

1/2 tsp red pepper flakes

1 tsp salt

1 lb fresh, ripe plum tomatoes, cored and chopped, and peeled and seeded if desired (or substitute 14.5 oz can diced tomatoes)

1 cup heavy cream, divided

1/2 cup grated Parmesan cheese, plus more to serve

1 Tbsp lemon juice

3 Tbsp minced parsley

salt and pepper

Cook pasta until al dente. Scoop out a cup of water and reserve, then drain the pasta.

Heat butter and olive oil in a large skillet over medium-high heat. Add cauliflower, toss to coat, and cook for 5 or so minutes, stirring occasionally. When florets are browned around the edges, add the garlic with its water, pepper flakes, and a teaspoon of salt. Cook for a minute or so, then add tomatoes and toss. Sauté for a few more minutes to cook off some of the moisture from the tomatoes.

Add 3/4 cup cream, bring to a simmer, and turn heat to low. Let sauce cook down for about 5 minutes. Add remaining 1/4 cup cream, drained pasta, Parmesan cheese, lemon juice, minced parsley, and black pepper to skillet (still over low heat). Toss gently. Taste for salt, pepper, and consistency. If sauce is too thick, add some saved pasta water. Serve with more Parmesan cheese.

Cauliflower

My Norwegian mother often served members of the cabbage family at meals, as these vegetables are a central part of Nordic cooking. Cauliflower was one of my favorites. It is less cabbage-y than, well, cabbage, and is just as versatile as broccoli. I have been surprised by the number of New Englanders who avoid this vegetable. I suspect they have mostly eaten it boiled or steamed, which tends to make it mushy. To those people, I have two words: Roast it. You will become a convert.

Chicken with Roasted Cauliflower

Brining is a great way to get moist chicken, but it requires some advance planning. This recipe allows you to skip brining but still get juicy chicken. It's adapted from food writer Michael Ruhlman, and can be used on days when you haven't planned ahead. The cauliflower and chicken roast at the same time in the oven.

SERVES **6** TO **8**

For the chicken

1 whole chicken (3 to 4 lbs; larger ones will take longer), rinsed and at room temperature

1 onion, quartered

2 tsp salt and 1/2 tsp black pepper, mixed in a small dish

2 Tbsp melted butter or olive oil

fresh thyme, rosemary, parsley, or other herbs, minced (optional)

For the cauliflower

2 heads cauliflower, outer leaves removed

2 Tbsp olive oil

salt and pepper

optional additions: chopped olives, chopped herbs, grated sharp cheese, capers

Preheat oven to 450 degrees. You can lower the temperature to 425 if you are worried about smoke, but a hotter oven makes a tastier chicken. Adjust your oven racks so the upper one has room to house a chicken. Prepare an ovenproof skillet for roasting the chicken. A well-seasoned iron skillet will be fine as is, but a stainless-steel skillet may need a brushing of canola oil on its surface.

Pat chicken dry with paper towels. Cut off the wing tips and freeze for use in stock, if you're inclined that way. Stuff the onion quarters into the chicken cavity. If you know how, truss the chicken. If you don't, leave as is.

Season the exterior of the chicken well with salt and pepper. Put it breast side up in the prepared skillet and place in oven on top rack.

After 30 minutes, remove chicken. (While you have the skillet out of the oven, place a potholder on the skillet handle so you remember not to touch it with your bare hand!) If you are using herbs, mix them with the butter or oil. Brush the chicken with the mixture, then return to oven.

After 30 more minutes, remove chicken and check for doneness. You can either check a small amount of internal juices (they should be clear, not red), or use an instant-read thermometer. The temperature in the thickest part of the thigh should read 170 degrees. If not done, return to oven and check in 5 minutes. Remove chicken and move to a serving plate. Tent with aluminum foil and let sit for a full 15 minutes. Don't cheat! A rested chicken is a moister chicken, as it allows time for the interior juices to redistribute, and you will lose less moisture when you cut into the meat.

While the chicken roasts, prepare the cauliflower. Cut each head in half, then trim the base of the core to remove the thickest part. Cut the heads into 1/2-inch-thick slices. Put cauliflower on sheet pan with sides, drizzle with olive oil, and toss well. When chicken has about 10 minutes left to roast, slide pan into oven.

After you check the chicken's doneness, remove the cauliflower pan from oven. Sprinkle with salt and pepper, and toss. Return to oven for another 10 or 15 minutes, depending on how brown you like it. The cauliflower will cook for a total of 20 to 25 minutes.

Serve the carved chicken with the cauliflower on the side. If you are feeling fancy, fold some chopped olives, herbs, capers, grated or chunked cheese, or a mixture thereof into the serving bowl with the cauliflower.

ROASTING VEGETABLES

Roasted vegetables are, without exaggeration, millions of times tastier than boiled ones. The trick is to use a high heat so they brown (i.e., caramelize). When roasting vegetables, it is essential to have a sheet pan with rimmed edges. It is also best to wash your vegetables and let them dry as much as possible before putting them in the oven. Damp vegetables are more likely to steam than brown.

Ruby's Cucumbers with Yogurt

My husband Mark, nicknamed Ruby, would happily eat cucumbers and yogurt three meals a day. He's developed a quicker way to mix cucumbers with yogurt than most versions of this Greek dish, known as tzatziki, *which call for grating and draining the cucumber. Avoid substituting regular plain yogurt for Greek style, or the dish will be too thin. Vary herbs according to your taste and what you have available.*

SERVES 6 TO 8 AS A SIDE DISH

2 large cucumbers, peeled or unpeeled, cut in half lengthwise, seeded or not, to your taste

1/2 tsp salt

2 cups plain Greek yogurt

2 tsp chopped fresh oregano or 1/2 tsp dried

2 tsp chopped fresh thyme or 1/2 tsp dried

1 small garlic clove, finely minced

1 Tbsp lemon juice

1/2 tsp lemon zest

2 Tbsp extra virgin olive oil

salt and pepper

Cut cucumbers in half lengthwise again (you will now have quarters) and cut into 1/4-inch-thick slices. Put in serving bowl and toss with 1/2 teaspoon salt. Add yogurt, herbs, garlic, lemon juice, and lemon zest. Mix gently. Season to taste with salt and pepper and stir. Pour olive oil over mixture. Fold a few times to incorporate. Enjoy for breakfast with pita or another bread, or refrigerate and eat as a side dish.

Cucumbers

Cucumbers have a lot to recommend them. Some folks malign the vegetable because of its low nutritional value and waxy skin. (Fortunately, farmer's market cucumbers are rarely waxed.) I would say its crunchiness outweighs all negatives, not to mention that cucumber is quick to prepare and makes a handy side dish. There are a number of varieties of cucumber, although they generally fall into ones that are good to pickle and ones that are not. In the following recipes, you can use any kind you have on hand.

Fried Haddock with Sweet-and-Sour Cucumber Salad

My Norwegian mother often accompanies fried or poached fish with a cucumber salad, although the salad also goes well with meat. In her words, though, "Meat is meat, but fish is food."

SERVES 4 TO 6

For the salad
3/4 cup white or rice vinegar

1/2 cup water

1 1/2 Tbsp white sugar

1 tsp salt

2 cucumbers, peeled if the skin is bumpy or thick, and seeded if you desire

For the haddock
1 1/2 cups flour

1 1/2 tsp salt

1/2 tsp pepper

2 lbs haddock fillets

2 oz butter or canola oil

lemon wedges and parsley for serving

Salad
Put the vinegar, water, sugar, and salt in a small pot. Bring just to boil, then remove from heat and cool. If you like extra zip, throw in a few whole black peppercorns.

Slice cucumber thinly. Place in serving bowl and cover with cooled vinegar mixture. Let dish sit at least 30 minutes before serving, to allow flavors to blend.

Haddock
Preheat oven to 200 degrees, and have an ovenproof plate ready. Mix the flour, salt, and pepper in a pie dish or other flat bowl. If the fish fillets are wide, cut them in half crosswise.

Melt the butter or oil in a large frying pan over medium-high heat. **A note about frying fish in butter:** *The butter will brown, which can be alarming, but it's much tastier than frying in canola oil.*

When the butter foams, dip one fillet at a time in the flour, coating both sides. Place fillets in pan without overcrowding. You will fry in at least two batches. Let fillets fry undisturbed for 2 to 3 minutes, then flip. They should be nice and brown. Finish fillets for another 2 to 3 minutes. Place on an ovenproof plate and keep warm in the oven until all pieces are fried, adding more fat to pan as needed. (Haddock is a lean fish and will stick without enough fat.)

Serve with lemon wedges and parsley sprigs. Spritz fish with additional lemon juice before eating. Leftovers make excellent sandwiches the next day.

CUCUMBER SURPRISE
Every so often a farmer's market or homegrown cucumber will give you a bitter mouthful. The culprit is a naturally occurring compound, although no one knows exactly why it sometimes occurs to excess. To avoid serving a bitter cuke, trim the stem end, which tends to harbor most of the compound, and take a little bite to taste. If the stem end tastes bitter, keep cutting slices off the cucumber from that end, until you reach a part which tastes good. Some people claim that salting the cucumber slices will remove the bitter taste, but that has never worked for me.

Broiled Eggplant Dip

This chunky dip is similar to the Middle Eastern dip, baba ghanoush, but omits the tahini. This recipe calls for mayonnaise as a binder. You can use the sesame seed paste instead, if you prefer, but you'll want to use a food processor to really incorporate it, and the texture will be much smoother. I like my eggplant broiled, but you can you can cube it and boil it if you want to hurry things along.

SERVES **4** TO **6** AS AN APPETIZER

1 large eggplant or several small ones

1 clove garlic, minced or pressed

1 tsp honey

1/2 tsp salt

1/4 tsp pepper

1/2 tsp cumin

1 to 2 Tbsp mayonnaise, to taste

2 tsp red wine vinegar

extra virgin olive oil

minced green herbs of your choice (e.g., chives, parsley, cilantro)

Preheat your broiler and line a rimmed baking sheet with foil. Wash the eggplant and prick it with a fork five or six times. Place it on the sheet and slide it onto the top rack of the oven. After 15 minutes, take eggplant out and turn it over. The skin should be charring; that's good. Return eggplant to oven.

Start checking for doneness after another 15 minutes. The vegetable needs to be collapsing, the flesh soft and pulling away from the skin in places. Depending on the size of the eggplant and strength of the broiler, this could take up to 45 minutes total.

Cut the cooked eggplant in half and dump it in a colander set in the sink, allowing liquid to drain. Let cool until ready to handle. Pull off the skin and place the flesh in a medium bowl. Add garlic, honey, salt, pepper, and cumin, and mash with a potato masher or fork. Stir in mayonnaise, then vinegar. Transfer to serving dish, drizzle with a little olive oil, and sprinkle with minced herbs. Serve with flatbread or crackers.

Eggplant

Although the result is delicious, frying eggplant takes work and a lot of oil. The recipes here rely on broiling or grilling instead. In many regions, eggplant is a midsummer vegetable, but in Maine it ripens in late summer or early fall. At that point, having the broiler on for an hour isn't a dreadful prospect. This is handy, because although broiling an eggplant until it collapses takes time, it is easy and provides a smoky base for dips and spreads. There are a variety of eggplants available at farmer's markets. They have a similar taste, but the smaller, thinner ones are sometimes more intense in flavor. The larger ones are easier to grill. Any variety will work here.

Grilled Eggplant Sandwich

This is a nice, quick supper to cook outside when you don't feel like heating up the kitchen. Add a side of potato salad and a cold beer, and you're all set.

SERVES **4**

2 Tbsp extra virgin olive oil, plus more for brushing

1 Tbsp red wine vinegar

1/2 tsp (generous) Dijon mustard

1 dozen Kalamata or Niçoise olives, pitted and chopped

2 handfuls of arugula or young Asian greens, washed, dried, and torn

8 thick slices sturdy bread, like sourdough or rustic French

1 good-size eggplant, or several small ones, unpeeled, cut into 1/4-inch-thick slices

4 slices of a large tomato

8 thin slices of red onion

3 oz chèvre-style goat cheese, crumbled

salt and pepper

Preheat outdoor grill to high. Mix olive oil, vinegar, and mustard in a medium bowl; otherwise arugula won't fit and whisk briefly to emulsify. Add olives and arugula and toss to coat. Season to taste with salt and pepper.

Lay the pieces of bread on a sheet pan and brush one side with a little olive oil. Set aside.

Brush both sides of the eggplant slices with olive oil and grill 3 to 4 minutes per side. The interior should be tender but not dried out and limp, so take a taste to be sure. Remove.

Place the bread slices oiled-side down on the grill for 1 or 2 minutes, enough to toast them.

To assemble the sandwiches: Take four slices of the bread and place them with the untoasted side up. Place a tomato slice and two slices of onion on each. Add a few eggplant slices. Cover each sandwich with one-quarter of the dressed greens, and crumble one-quarter of the cheese on top. Place second slice of bread on top, toasted side up, and press together firmly.

Lemony Spinach and Quinoa Soup

Quinoa has a nutty taste, cooks quickly, and packs a big nutritional punch It's not grown in New England, but at least it originates in the New World.

SERVES **6**

2 Tbsp olive oil

1 Tbsp butter

1/2 medium yellow onion, diced

1 1/2 tsp salt, divided

12 oz button mushrooms cut into 1/4-inch-thick slices, or broken into pieces

1 lemon

2 garlic cloves, minced or pressed

1 tsp dried thyme

1/2 tsp smoked paprika

1/4 tsp sugar

1/4 tsp allspice

12 oz potatoes (about two medium), peeled and diced into 1/2-inch cubes

5 cups water

3/4 cup quinoa

2 small bunches or 1 big bunch spinach, stemmed, washed, and torn into pieces (about 8 cups)

salt and pepper

Greek yogurt for serving (optional)

Heat olive oil and butter in a large saucepan over medium heat. When foaming subsides, add onion and 1 teaspoon salt. Cook until softened, about 5 minutes. Raise heat to high and add mushrooms. Cook, stirring regularly, until the liquid from the mushrooms has evaporated and bottom is beginning to brown, about 6 minutes.

While mushrooms are cooking, remove three long strips of skin from the lemon with a vegetable peeler. Try to get the yellow part only and avoid the white pith. Put the minced garlic, thyme, smoked paprika, sugar, and allspice in a small bowl with a tablespoon of water. Keep the lemon on hand for juicing.

When mushrooms are done cooking, reduce heat to medium. Clear a spot in the center of the pot and add lemon strips and garlic mixture. Stir to combine, then tip in the potatoes, and stir gently.

Add water and bring to a boil. Add quinoa and 1/2 teaspoon salt, and reduce to a simmer. Partially cover saucepan and simmer soup for 15 minutes. Test to see if potatoes are tender and quinoa is cooked through; continue simmering if need be. When cooked, remove lemon strips. Add spinach, a tablespoon of lemon juice from the lemon, and salt and pepper to taste. Stir for a few seconds to help spinach wilt. Remove from heat and adjust seasonings.

Serve topped with a dollop of Greek yogurt in each dish.

Spinach

Unfortunately, whenever I think about spinach, I hear in my head, "We hate spinach! We hate spinach!" This is because I once heard the line in a puppet show, and it's never left my consciousness. I actually love spinach. Spinach is versatile and can be quickly sautéed and flavored in a variety of ways (with lemon, garlic, hot pepper) to make an easy and nutritious side dish. Young, tender spinach can be tossed into salads, but don't try this with mature, tougher spinach unless you want to spend a lot of time chewing. The substantial, curly spinach is more flavorful and does well in longer-cooking preparations.

Spinach and Grape Salad

This recipe works well as a late-summer main dish or as a side salad. If you can't find local grapes, you can substitute chunks of watermelon.

SERVES **6** AS A SIDE SALAD

3/4 cup walnuts, coarsely chopped

2 medium tomatoes, cored, cut into wedges

1 tsp salt, divided

2 Tbsp extra virgin olive oil

1 Tbsp red wine vinegar

1 small clove garlic, minced

1 tsp honey

1/2 tsp smoked paprika

1/2 tsp oregano

1/4 tsp black pepper

1 small cucumber, peeled or unpeeled, halved lengthwise

2 bunches baby spinach, stemmed and washed (about 6 cups)

1 cup Concord grapes, halved

3/4 cup feta cheese, crumbled

Heat oven to 350 degrees. Put walnuts on a sheet pan and place in oven. Toast for 8 minutes, or until browned. Remove and let cool.

Place tomatoes in a large salad bowl and sprinkle with 1/2 teaspoon salt. Let sit while you make the dressing.

Combine olive oil, vinegar, garlic, honey, paprika, oregano, 1/2 teaspoon salt, and pepper in a small bowl. Whisk well to emulsify.

Cut cucumber in half lengthwise again. Slice into 1/2-inch-thick chunks. Add cucumber, spinach, grapes, and feta to salad bowl. Whisk dressing again to emulsify, then pour over ingredients and toss, stirring from the bottom to get the tomato juices. Top with walnuts.

Zucchini and Eggplant Casserole

Because of the rice, this casserole can work as a main dish as well as a side. You can substitute summer squash for the zucchini if that's what you have on hand.

SERVES **8** AS A SIDE DISH

4 medium or 2 large zucchini

2 tsp salt, divided

olive oil for casserole dish

3 eggs

1 cup crumbled feta cheese

1 1/4 cups grated Parmesan cheese, divided

1 Tbsp lemon juice

1 clove garlic, minced or pressed

2 Tbsp minced parsley or cilantro

1 tsp smoked paprika

1 tsp cumin

generous pinch cayenne

1/4 tsp sugar

1/2 tsp black pepper

1/2 cup uncooked white rice

2 eggplant, broiled, drained, and roughly chopped (for method, see **Broiled Eggplant Dip** recipe on page 7)

1 or 2 tomatoes, sliced

1 or 2 Tbsp extra virgin olive oil

Preheat oven to 375 degrees. Grate the zucchini on the large holes of a box grater, or with grating disk of a food processor. Put in a bowl, sprinkle with 1 teaspoon salt, and toss. Let sit while you prepare the remainder of the recipe.

Coat a medium-size shallow casserole dish with olive oil.

Crack eggs into a large mixing bowl and beat lightly. Add the feta, about two-thirds of the Parmesan cheese, lemon juice, garlic, parsley, spices, sugar, 1 teaspoon salt, and pepper, and mix well. Add rice and eggplant and combine.

Lift the zucchini out of its bowl by large fistfuls, and gently squeeze out excess water. You don't need to remove every last drop of water, because the rice will absorb liquid while cooking. Add the squeezed zucchini to the egg mixture. Stir and adjust seasoning to taste.

Pour mixture into the prepared dish and bake for 20 minutes. Meanwhile, salt the sliced tomatoes and place them on paper towels to absorb moisture. Remove the casserole from oven, top with sliced tomatoes and remaining Parmesan cheese, drizzle with extra virgin olive oil, and return to oven for an additional 20 minutes. Let stand 5 minutes before serving.

Summer Squash

The running joke about summer squash (that is, zucchini and its relatives) is that everybody grows it and nobody wants all they grow. I was never a big fan of summer squash and have often made fun of my neighbor Lewis for growing so much of it in his small garden. Only lately have I discovered the great uses for this vegetable. Roasting summer squash transforms it into a delicious side dish. I've also fallen in love with Jim Lahey's recipe for zucchini pizza. (Lahey is the baker who popularized the "no-knead" bread recipe a few years ago.) I often use his technique for prepping zucchini (as in the casserole below). In most recipes, you can use zucchini and summer squash interchangeably, depending on what you have on hand.

Pasta with Summer Squash and Caramelized Onions

I used to think caramelizing onions was hard and only for professionals. It's actually easy; it takes time but not much attention. This dish includes a lot of soft textures— soft roasted squash, soft caramelized onions, soft ricotta cheese—something to think about if you don't care for soft pasta. Also, it may seem like a lot of squash, but it cooks down considerably.

SERVES **6**

3 medium summer squash, ends trimmed

4 Tbsp olive oil, divided

1 tsp salt, divided

1/4 tsp pepper

1/2 cup pine nuts or chopped walnuts

1 Tbsp butter

2 yellow onions, halved crosswise and cut into 1/3-inch-thick slices

1 Tbsp balsamic vinegar

12 oz bowtie pasta

3/4 cup fresh ricotta

2 Tbsp chopped basil

salt and pepper

1/2 cup grated Parmesan cheese, plus more to serve

Preheat oven to 425 degrees. Prepare the squash by cutting them in half lengthwise. Slice the smaller neck sections into 3/4-inch-thick half-moons. Halve the thick bodies of the squash lengthwise again, then cut into 3/4-inch-thick slices. Spread squash on a rimmed sheet pan and drizzle with 3 tablespoons olive oil. Roast 15 minutes in oven.

Remove, season with 1/2 teaspoon salt and 1/4 teaspoon pepper, stir with a spatula, and return to oven for another 15 minutes, until very soft and browned in spots. Set aside.

Put nuts in separate pan and add to oven. Toast for 2 or 3 minutes, until lightly browned and fragrant. Remove and let cool.

Meanwhile, heat remaining tablespoon olive oil and butter in a medium skillet over medium-high heat. When foaming dies down, add onion slices and toss. Cook over medium-high heat, stirring occasionally, until the onions begin to brown. Season with 1/2 teaspoon salt and stir well, scraping the bottom of the pan to make sure no onions stick. Turn heat to medium-low and cook, stirring often, until all the onion slices are soft, sweet, and brown. If you notice the onions getting dry or sticking, add a tablespoon of water. It will probably take about 30 minutes to get them fully brown. Stir in vinegar and remove from heat.

Boil pasta until al dente. Scoop out a cup of pasta water, then drain the pasta. Put ricotta in the bottom of the serving bowl and whisk in a few spoonfuls of the hot pasta water to make the cheese creamy and smooth. Add pasta, roasted squash, onions, basil, grated Parmesan, and a good grind of pepper. Fold to combine. Adjust seasonings. Sprinkle walnuts on top. Serve with Parmesan cheese.

October

brussels sprouts

raspberries

parsley

kohlrabi

pears

October

FEATURED INGREDIENTS

Brussels Sprouts,
Kohlrabi,
Parsley,
Pears,
Raspberries

FOR MOST OF NEW ENGLAND, the first hard frost, when temperatures drop to freezing or below, arrives this month. While hardy crops like kale and broccoli can survive, October spells the end for all summery vegetables not grown in hothouses or trucked in from warmer climes. It also means the beginning of our culinary friendship with members of the cabbage family, which not only persist in cold weather but also store well.

October also brings the last of fresh fruit from the region. A second crop of raspberries is usually in, although you have to get to the farmer's market early if you want to snag them. Pears appear, but it's apples that dominate New England's fruit bins.

This is the best time for eating an apple out of hand, and by this time there is a variety for everyone—crisp, soft, tart, sweet, juicy. Unlike apples, pears do not store well, so enjoy them during their short, seasonal appearance. You won't find as many varieties as apples, but there are differences, from juicy Bartletts to crisp Asian pears.

Maple-Roasted Brussels Sprouts

Maple syrup is a great foil to the slight bitterness of Brussels sprouts.

SERVES **4** AS A SIDE DISH

6 cups Brussels sprouts
(about 1 1/2 lbs), washed
and trimmed

3 Tbsp maple syrup,
plus more to serve

1 Tbsp prepared mustard
(Dijon or whole-grain)

2 Tbsp olive oil

1 tsp salt

1/2 tsp black pepper

lemon juice, to taste

Preheat oven to 425 degrees. Halve any Brussels sprouts larger than 1 1/2 inches in diameter.

Place 3 tablespoons maple syrup, mustard, olive oil, salt, and pepper in a medium bowl and whisk together. Add sprouts to bowl and toss to coat. Pour coated sprouts onto a rimmed sheet pan, using a spatula to scrape out any extra sauce.

Roast for 15 minutes, stir, and roast another 10 minutes. Check to see if sprouts are done. They should be browned in spots and tender to the bite. Cook longer if necessary. Put cooked sprouts in a serving bowl and toss with a drizzle of maple syrup and lemon juice. Salt to taste.

Brussels Sprouts

Brussels sprouts may be the most surprising member of the cabbage family. In the supermarket, they are mounds of lumpy green spheres, but at the farmer's market, the globes are often sold sticking out of their thick green stalks, like a magic wand from some alien giant wizard. I never touched Brussels sprouts as a child, probably because in the 1970s, they were boiled until mushy and watery. To my surprise, they have become one of my kids' favorite vegetables. Of course, the boys get them roasted, usually with maple syrup. And they get the satisfaction of eating an entire mini-head of cabbage at once. Maybe they enjoy pretending to be giants.

Kohlrabi and Brussels Sprouts Salad

Raw Brussels sprouts are quite tasty, but they really need to be shaved thinly, as their texture is a bit chewy. Because of how small they are, the best way to shred them is with the slicing or grating disk of a food processor. If you are confident, you can also use a mandoline.

SERVES **6** AS A SIDE SALAD

1/3 cup hazelnuts

5 Tbsp extra virgin olive oil

1 Tbsp lemon juice

2 Tbsp balsamic vinegar

1/2 tsp honey

salt and pepper

2 Tbsp minced parsley

2 cups Brussels sprouts (about 3/4 lb), trimmed and shredded

2 medium kohlrabi bulbs, peeled, root end removed

1/2 medium apple, peeled, cored, and diced

1 medium carrot, sliced into 1/8-inch-thick coins

1 green onion, green part sliced thinly

Preheat oven to 350 degrees. Put hazelnuts on a tray and toast for 8 to 12 minutes, depending on how toasted you like them. Remove and cool. If nuts have skins, you can remove most of them simply by rubbing the nuts against each other. Chop coarsely.

To make the dressing, pour olive oil into a small bowl. Briskly whisk in lemon juice, vinegar, honey, salt, and pepper. Stir in parsley.

Put shredded Brussels sprouts in a serving bowl. Shred one kohlrabi bulb and add to bowl. Cut remaining kohlrabi into 3/4-inch dice, and add to bowl with apple, carrot, and green onion. Pour dressing over and toss. Add salt and pepper to taste. Sprinkle hazelnuts on top.

Mashed Potatoes and Kohlrabi

Kohlrabi can be mashed on its own, but it has a tendency to be a bit watery. Mixing it with potatoes bulks up the kohlrabi and cuts down on the starchiness of the potatoes. Note that kohlrabi can get fibrous, especially if the bulbs are large, so make sure when prepping them to fully remove the core near the root end.

SERVES 4 AS A SIDE DISH

3 medium bulbs kohlrabi, peeled, with root end removed, cut into 1 1/2-inch chunks

2 large potatoes, peeled, cut into 1 1/2-inch chunks

1/4 cup cream

3 Tbsp butter, divided

salt and pepper

Put prepared kohlrabi in a large saucepan and add water just to cover. Add 2 teaspoons salt, bring to a boil, and cook for 10 minutes. Add potatoes and continue boiling until potatoes and kohlrabi are soft, about another 15 minutes. Drain in a large colander, then return to the saucepan over low heat. Stir to let any remaining water evaporate, then add cream and 2 tablespoons of the butter. Stir to coat, and heat until butter has melted. Mash with a potato masher; if you want a very smooth consistency, pass through a ricer. Add salt and pepper to taste. Serve with remaining tablespoon of butter melting on top.

Kohlrabi

The name alone seems implausible. Then when you see the vegetable, your suspicions are confirmed: Kohlrabi is from another planet. Actually, it's from Germany, or somewhere in Europe, and it's another member of the cabbage family. It's very easy to grow and enjoys worldwide popularity, especially in the Indian subcontinent. If you were to search the Internet for kohlrabi and Kashmir, you would find a host of curry-based recipes to try. Here in the United States, kohlrabi is considered mysterious. Like green or red cabbage, kohlrabi is enjoyable in its raw, crunchy state as well as cooked. Some recipes seek to disguise its connection to cabbage. I've heard of people dicing it and sautéing the vegetable with butter, salt, and a little sugar to give it a taste and texture resembling something like sweet corn. But I like its flavor as is. It's like a cross between a cabbage and a mild turnip.

Lemon Chard Kohlrabi

You don't actually need the chard for this to be tasty, although the leaves do provide a nice contrast with the kohlrabi.

SERVES **6** AS A SIDE DISH

3 Tbsp olive oil

1 medium or large bulb kohlrabi, peeled, with root end removed, cut into 1/4-inch sticks

salt

1 lemon, zested and juiced

1 bunch chard, washed well

3 cloves garlic, sliced

1/4 tsp red pepper flakes

black pepper

Heat the olive oil in a large skillet over medium-high heat. Add kohlrabi, 1/2 teaspoon salt, and 1 tablespoon of lemon juice and stir to coat. Sauté, stirring occasionally, for 5 minutes, until somewhat tender.

While the kohlrabi cooks, prepare the chard. Cut the stems into 1/4-inch-thick pieces. Cut chard leaves in half lengthwise, down the rib; cut any large leaves again lengthwise. Then cut the leaves into 1-inch-wide strips.

Add chard stems to pan and cook 5 minutes; add chard leaves. Sprinkle with 1/4 teaspoon salt, stir, and sauté, stirring occasionally, until leaves have cooked down, about 4 or 5 minutes.

Push vegetables to side of the pan. Add garlic, red pepper, lemon zest, and remaining lemon juice to the middle of the pan. Let sizzle, stirring gently, until fragrant—about 30 seconds. Mix vegetables and seasonings together, cook for an additional minute, and remove from heat. Season with salt and black pepper to taste.

Parsley and Barley Soup

Barley is a thirsty grain. This soup will thicken after being made, so feel free to add more water to thin it. You can simplify the recipe by leaving out the potato and turnip and adding more carrots. Really, you can use any root vegetables you have on hand—just make sure they come to about two cups when chopped.

SERVES **4** TO **6**

1 Tbsp olive oil

3 slices bacon, finely diced

1 carrot, sliced into 1/4-inch coins

1 large bunch parsley, stems removed* and divided as follows: 1/2 cup coarsely chopped, and 1 cup (or more) finely chopped

1/2 tsp sugar

3 cloves garlic, smashed

2 Tbsp tomato paste

1 potato, chopped into 3/4-inch cubes

1 turnip, chopped into 3/4-inch cubes

3/4 cup pearl barley

4 cups vegetable broth or chicken broth or water

1 to 3 Tbsp sherry vinegar or cider vinegar (to taste)

salt and pepper

Parmesan cheese, for serving (optional)

Heat olive oil and bacon in a soup pot over medium heat. Cook bacon for 5 minutes, stirring often, then add carrot, 1/2 cup of coarsely chopped parsley, sugar, and 1/2 teaspoon salt. Stirring regularly, sauté for about 5 minutes. The bacon should be browned and fairly crisp. Add garlic, cook 30 seconds, then add tomato paste and stir well, cooking for another 30 seconds. The bottom of the pot should be getting quite brown; this is good. Just don't let it turn black; if it's browning too fast, lower the heat.

Add the potato, turnip, and barley. Stir to combine. Add water or broth. Stir, scraping up the brown bits stuck to the bottom of the pan. Bring the mixture to a boil. Turn heat to low, cover, and simmer until the barley and root vegetables are tender, about 30 minutes.

Add finely chopped parsley and cook a few more minutes, until wilted. Add vinegar. Season with salt and pepper to taste. Serve with grated Parmesan cheese and more minced parsley, if desired.

Note: *If you really love parsley, you can add the stems to the water or broth before adding the liquid to the soup pot. This will add another note of parsley flavor to the soup. To do this, heat the liquid and stems together, then strain the liquid into the barley mixture. Discard the stems.*

Parsley

In cold Norway, where my mother is from, parsley is considered a green vegetable. A plate of white food, like poached fish and boiled potatoes, often includes a few sprigs of parsley as the vegetable on the plate. But other cultures use parsley in copious quantities and far more creative ways. Countries of the Mediterranean and Middle East have excellent dishes that use the herb as a major part of a meal. Nutritionally, parsley contains good amounts of vitamins K and C, as well as some vitamin A and even iron. Who knew that this little sprig could do so much?

Grilled Steak with Parsley Sauce

This sauce is a version of chimichurri. People feel strongly about this Argentine sauce, and I would never argue that this recipe is authentic. I just like it. The quantities in this recipe work well in a food processor, which needs a certain volume to be effective, and will leave you with plenty of extra. If you are making it by hand, you may wish to halve the recipe. With its anchovies and raw garlic, this sauce will, as an old family friend used to say, put hair on your chest.

For the parsley sauce
MAKES **1 1/2** CUPS

2 cups parsley leaves, chopped

2 Tbsp chopped green onions or garlic scapes

4 cloves garlic, smashed

1 tsp salt

1/2 cup extra virgin olive oil

1/4 cup red wine vinegar

5 anchovy fillets, chopped

1 Tbsp lemon juice

1 tsp smoked paprika

1/4 tsp red pepper flakes

1/4 cup water, boiling

For the steak
MAKES SIX **4**-OUNCE SERVINGS

1 1/2 lbs strip steak (or your favorite grill-friendly cut)

salt and pepper

Parsley sauce

Place all ingredients except water into a food processor. Give the mixture five 1-second pulses. Scrape down the bowl and pulse again five times. Leaving processor on, pour hot water gradually into mixture as it whirls. When fully incorporated, remove from processor and adjust seasoning.

To make by hand, chop parsley, onions, garlic, and anchovies finely and combine in a bowl with remaining ingredients except water. Pour hot water over while stirring briskly. Adjust seasoning to taste.

Note: *The sauce, when first made, may seem a bit runny. The consistency will firm up noticeably as it rests.*

Steak

Food scientists like J. Kenji López-Alt have shown that when to salt a steak is key to improving flavor and juiciness. If you can prepare your steak well in advance, salt it heavily the day before and leave it uncovered in the refrigerator. If you have less time, salt the steak heavily but let it rest outside of the refrigerator for 40 minutes. If you have even less time, let the meat come to room temperature and salt it just before cooking. In all cases, season with pepper right before it goes on the grill.

Preheat grill so that one side is very hot and the other is at low heat. Start steak on the low-heat side, and grill to your preferred doneness, flipping regularly. Timing will depend on the thickness of your steak. The easiest way to check for doneness is with an instant-read thermometer, using 120 degrees for rare, 140 for medium, and 160 for well done. When your meat is ready, switch it to the hotter side of the grill and sear it for a minute or two per side. Remove from heat and let it rest for a few minutes.

Serve with parsley sauce slathered on top, and with bread on the side for dipping into the sauce.

SEASONING RAW MEAT

Recipes often call for seasoning raw meat with salt and pepper on both sides before cooking, but that requires a lot of hand washing if you don't want to leave traces of raw meat on your salt shaker and pepper grinder. To make things easier, fill a small bowl with a mixture of salt and pepper (I like a three-to-one ratio). When you need to season your meat, you can use your unwashed hands to pinch the seasoning out of the bowl. (Although bacteria probably cannot survive long in such a salty environment, you may want to discard the mix when you are done.)

Parsley Risotto

Risotto is very adaptable. My father tended to plant too much parsley in his garden, so he often asked me to make parsley risotto, with chocolate pudding for dessert.

SERVES **4** AS A SMALL MAIN COURSE

4 1/2 cups vegetable or
chicken broth (approximately)

2 Tbsp butter, divided

1 Tbsp olive oil

1 shallot, diced

1 1/2 cups parsley, finely
chopped and divided

salt

2 cups arborio rice

1/2 cup white wine or vermouth

1/3 cup Parmesan cheese

1/2 tsp lemon zest

2 tsp lemon juice

1/2 tsp pepper

1 1/2 cups green peas
(frozen is fine)

1/2 cup feta cheese, crumbled,
plus more for serving

Heat the broth in a small saucepan. Once it boils, turn heat to low, and leave the broth on the burner to keep it warm.

Heat 1 tablespoon butter and the olive oil in a medium saucepan over medium heat. When foaming subsides, add the shallot, 1/2 cup of the parsley, and 1/2 teaspoon salt. Cook 2 minutes, then add the rice, and stir to coat. Cook rice for 2 minutes, stirring frequently. Add wine and cook, again stirring frequently, until the wine is almost gone. Add 2 cups of warm broth and stir vigorously. Bring to a boil. Reduce heat, keeping the mixture simmering at a medium clip. Cook, uncovered, stirring regularly and vigorously until the liquid evaporates.

Add the remainder of the broth to the rice one ladleful (about 1/4 cup) at a time. (If you run out of broth, add heated water.) Each time you add broth, stir well and wait until the liquid evaporates before adding more. Continue this process until rice is cooked to just a little bit less than your desired texture (residual heat will finish cooking it). Total cooking time will be around 20 minutes. Add one last small ladleful of broth, and remove from heat.

Add Parmesan cheese, lemon zest and juice, pepper, remaining table-spoon butter, peas, and feta cheese. Stir well to incorporate, cover, and let sit a few minutes. Add last cup of parsley, stirring well. Serve with more Parmesan or feta, to taste.

Green Salad with Pears

You can swap out many of these ingredients—walnuts for the pecans, dried cherries for the cranberries, shaved Parmesan cheese for the blue cheese. Use whatever feels right to you.

SERVES **4**

3/4 cup pecans, coarsely chopped

2 cups arugula or other spicy green

4 cups lettuce, washed and torn

1 cucumber, thinly sliced

1/4 cup olive oil

2 Tbsp rice vinegar

1 Tbsp minced shallot or chives

1 tsp Dijon mustard

1 tsp honey or maple syrup

1/2 tsp salt

pepper

3 pears, unpeeled, cored, and cut into eighths

1/3 cup dried cranberries

1/3 cup crumbled blue cheese

Preheat oven to 350 degrees and toast pecans on a sheet pan for about 8 minutes, until fragrant. Cool.

Place greens and cucumber in a salad bowl. Whisk together olive oil, vinegar, shallot, mustard, honey, salt, and pepper to taste in a small bowl. Pour over greens and cucumber and toss. Add pecans, pears, and cranberries, and toss gently. Top with blue cheese.

Pears

Pears are not a huge crop in New England. Although pear trees, especially Bartletts, can tolerate the cold, most varieties do better with more temperate weather. There are probably ten or twenty acres devoted to apples in New England for every acre devoted to pears. This is too bad, because a ripe, juicy pear is one of life's great pleasures. An Italian proverb says "Al contadino non far sapere quant'é buono il formaggio con le pere." Translation: "The farmer doesn't get to know how good cheese is with pears." This implies a sort of craftiness on the part of consumers, trying to get the farmer to produce pears without letting on how delicious they are when eaten on a fruit and cheese plate. Maybe New England farmers haven't fallen for this trick and aren't growing very many pears out of spite.

Skillet Chicken with Pears and Brussels Sprouts

You may need to fiddle with the cooking time for the pears, depending on how big they are. I find skinless and boneless chicken works best in this recipe, but you can also use bone-in chicken parts, if that's what you have; just adjust the cooking time accordingly.

SERVES **4**

For the herbed butter
3 Tbsp butter, cut into chunks and at room temperature

2 Tbsp finely chopped herbs (chives, basil, parsley, or a combination)

1/2 tsp lemon zest

1/4 tsp salt

1/4 tsp pepper

For the chicken
1 1/2 lbs boneless, skinless chicken parts (thighs work well), trimmed of excess fat

salt and pepper

1 Tbsp plus 1 tsp canola oil, divided

1/2 cup white wine or vermouth

1/4 cup chicken or vegetable broth or water

4 cups Brussels sprouts (about 1 lb), trimmed, and halved if larger than 1 1/2 inch in diameter

1 Tbsp butter

2 Tbsp maple syrup

2 firm pears, halved, cored, sliced 3/4-inch thick, with slices cut in half horizontally

Place butter in a small mixing bowl. Add remaining ingredients and mash together until thoroughly combined. Set aside.

Pat the chicken parts dry with a paper towel, and season both sides with salt and pepper. Heat 1 tablespoon oil in a large, sturdy skillet over medium heat. Add the chicken, wine, and broth and bring to a simmer. Reduce heat to low, cover, and simmer 5 minutes. Remove cover, increase heat to medium-high, and cook about 5 more minutes, until the chicken is barely cooked through (160 degrees by a meat thermometer). The exact time will depend on the thickness and cut of the chicken. Remove chicken to a large plate.

When the liquid in the skillet has mostly evaporated, add Brussels sprouts and 1/2 teaspoon salt and cook, stirring regularly, for 8 to 10 minutes, until nearly tender. If pan ever becomes dry during this process, add a tablespoon of water.

Push sprouts to the sides of the skillet. Reduce heat to medium. Add 1 tablespoon butter and the maple syrup to center. When butter has melted, add pears to skillet. Cook 4 or 5 minutes, stirring gently every so often, until pears are slightly browned and tender. Remove the pan from the heat, and move the pears and sprouts to a serving platter. Put a few teaspoons of the herbed butter on top of the pears and sprouts, and leave it to melt.

Return the pan to medium heat. Add the remaining teaspoon of oil to the pan. Return the chicken to the skillet and cook undisturbed for 1 to 2 minutes per side, to brown slightly and warm through. Put the chicken on the serving platter with the pears and sprouts, and top each piece of chicken with a dollop of the herbed butter.

A note about cleanup: *The sugars in the maple syrup make for a messy pan. I find it handy to soak the skillet in a little warm water while enjoying the meal. Then by cleanup time, the sugars stuck to the bottom of the pan should have dissolved.*

Brown Sugar Pear Cake

This is an upside-down fruitcake. You could substitute apples for the pears or throw in some cranberries if you have them. The recipe is a version of one popularized by expat pastry chef David Lebovitz, who writes a wonderful blog about his culinary adventures in France.

SERVES **10**

1 1/3 cups brown sugar, lightly packed, divided

11 Tbsp butter, divided

1 tsp salt, divided

1 tsp lemon juice

1/2 cup sliced almonds

3 firm pears (about 1 lb), cored and peeled, and sliced 3/4-inch thick

1 1/4 cups flour

1 1/2 tsp baking powder

1/2 tsp ginger

1/2 tsp cinnamon

1/2 cup sour cream

1 1/2 tsp vanilla

1 Tbsp brandy

2 eggs, room temperature if possible

Grease a 9-inch cake pan (not a springform) with sides at least 1 1/2 inches high. In a saucepan over medium heat, heat 2/3 cup of brown sugar, 3 tablespoons of the butter, 1/2 teaspoon of the salt, and lemon juice, stirring to combine. When mixture bubbles, remove from heat and pour into the prepared cake pan. Sprinkle almonds over the mix. Arrange pears on top, either in a nice, concentric circle, or in a jumble.

Preheat oven to 350 degrees.

Place flour, baking powder, remaining 1/2 teaspoon of salt, ginger, and cinnamon in a small bowl and stir to combine. Combine sour cream, vanilla, and brandy in a measuring cup.

In a mixing bowl on medium-low speed, cream the remaining 8 tablespoons butter for 1 minute. Add remaining 2/3 cup brown sugar and beat until fluffy. Increase speed to medium and add the eggs one at a time, combining well after each. (The mixture may look shaggy; don't worry.) Turn mixer off and scrape down the bowl. On low speed, add a third of the dry mixture. When it is mostly incorporated, add half of the sour cream mixture. Mix until mostly combined. Repeat. Then add last third of flour mixture and mix for 15 seconds. Stop the mixer and scrape down the bowl. On medium-high speed, mix for another 10 seconds, until the batter looks smooth. Spoon the batter on top of the pears, smoothing the top with a spatula.

Bake the cake for 35 minutes, then check for doneness. When a toothpick inserted into the cake part (not the fruit) comes out dry, it's ready. Do not underbake this cake; it must be fully baked to support the fruit. Cool the cake in the pan on a baking rack for 30 minutes to 1 hour. Place a serving plate on top of the cake pan and turn the cake upside down, letting it fall onto the plate. If some of the fruit mixture sticks to the pan, use a spatula to replace it on top of the cake. No one will notice. Serve the cake warm with whipped cream. Warmed-up leftovers are delicious for breakfast.

Spinach, Raspberry, and Goat Cheese Salad

Avoid tossing this salad much once the delicate raspberries have been added. I like including chopped toasted nuts, to give it a little bite. Hazelnuts are particularly good here. Or, if you're tired of toasted nuts, you could substitute some crunchy lettuce for some of the spinach.

SERVES **4** TO **6**

6 Tbsp extra virgin olive oil

1/4 cup red wine vinegar

1 tsp honey

2 Tbsp minced shallots

1/2 tsp dried thyme or 2 tsp fresh thyme leaves, minced

1/2 tsp salt

1/4 tsp black pepper

6 cups baby spinach leaves

1/2 red onion, sliced thinly

1/2 zucchini, sliced thinly

1 cup raspberries

1/2 cup (about 3 oz) of fresh, soft chèvre-style goat cheese

Whisk together the olive oil, vinegar, honey, shallots, thyme, salt, and pepper in a small bowl.

In a large serving bowl, combine the spinach, red onion, and zucchini. Pour dressing over and toss well to coat. Add the raspberries and goat cheese and toss gently.

Raspberries

I have heard it said that the best way to enjoy raspberries is to eat them with heavy cream and a sprinkle of sugar. I'm not going to disagree. My mother used to pick quantities of raspberries and make delicious, tart raspberry jam. Not everyone wants to put the time into such an endeavor. For the rest of us (and those of us skipping the heavy cream), putting raspberries into salads is an excellent way to eat them.

A big question about raspberries is whether to wash them or not. They are very delicate, and when doused with water can easily become soggy. The best advice I can give is after washing, make sure to dry them thoroughly. Either spread them out on paper towels and let them air-dry completely, or take a tip from Cook's Illustrated and put them on top of paper towels in a salad spinner. Then spin gently. Gently!

RASPBERRY VINAIGRETTE

In addition to tossing raspberries into salads, you can use them to make a dressing. I don't always like hauling out the blender to make a salad dressing, which you need to smooth out the berries, so I make extra and save some for later. For 1 cup of raspberries, use 2 tablespoons of white wine vinegar, 2 teaspoons of honey, and 1/4 teaspoon of salt. Blend until smooth, and then, with the blender on, slowly add 1/3 cup of extra virgin olive oil to emulsify the dressing. If your berries are particularly sweet or sour, you may want to vary the proportions of vinegar and honey accordingly.

Raspberry Yogurt Tart

This is a recipe from Julia Child that I adapted slightly. It's great for breakfast. You can always buy a piecrust or puff-pastry dough if you don't have time to make one from scratch. And it may be heresy, but a graham-cracker crust works too. Just fully prebake the crust.

SERVES **8**

1 11-inch **tart shell** (piecrust), fully baked (recipe follows)

2 eggs

1/3 cup sugar

1 2/3 cups plain, thick yogurt

1/4 tsp salt

1 Tbsp vanilla

1/4 cup flour

1 pint raspberries

Place a rimmed baking sheet in the oven and preheat oven to 325 degrees.

In a standing mixer, use whisk attachment to whip eggs and sugar until thickened and lightened, 2 to 3 minutes. Using a rubber spatula, gently stir in yogurt, salt, and vanilla. Put flour in a sifter and sift over mixture, then fold in. You want to avoid having any large blobs of dry flour, but don't worry if the mixture looks a little lumpy. Pour filling into prepared tart shell and smooth. Scatter berries over the top, and sprinkle a little sugar over the raspberries.

Place tart on preheated baking sheet. Bake 35 to 40 minutes, until the top is puffed and golden. Let cool at least 20 minutes before attempting to slice.

PRESERVING RASPBERRIES

The easiest way to save raspberries is to freeze them with sugar. Because the sugar absorbs extra moisture, you don't need to worry about drying the berries off completely after rinsing them. Gently mix 1/4 cup sugar with every 2 cups of berries and wait until sugar has dissolved. Freeze in resealable Ziploc bags.

To freeze without sugar, you first must dry the berries off completely after rinsing them (if you do rinse them; some people don't). Then spread the berries out on a parchment-lined baking sheet, making sure the berries don't touch. Freeze the entire sheet for several hours. When individual berries are frozen, remove them from the tray and pack them into resealable Ziploc bags. If you skip the step of laying the berries out separately, they will tend to clump together when frozen, which can make it harder to obtain specific portion sizes.

For the tart shell

1 1/2 cups flour

1 1/2 tsp sugar

1/2 tsp salt

4 Tbsp cold butter, in chunks

2 Tbsp plus 1 tsp shortening, chilled if possible

6 Tbsp cold buttermilk

cold water (as needed)

Tart shell

Put flour, sugar, and salt in the bowl of a food processor. Pulse once to combine. Drop butter on top and give six 1-second pulses. Drop shortening in and pulse six more times. Check consistency; there should be no chunks bigger than a pea. If needed, pulse a few more times. Pour buttermilk in and whirl for 5 seconds. If dough has not come together yet, add cold water 1 tablespoon at a time. Try not to add too much liquid; the dough will be relatively dry. Whirl briefly after each addition, stopping as soon as most of the dough starts forming a ball (some will still look like crumbs). Remove from food processor.

Wrap dough in plastic wrap, squeezing any looser parts together. Chill for an hour, if possible. Roll dough out to a 12-inch circle and press into an 11-inch tart pan. Make the sides of the tart extra high to accommodate any shrinking. Prick dough all over with a fork, then place it in the freezer. Turn oven to 425 degrees and place a baking sheet in oven.

When the oven is at 425 degrees, remove tart shell from freezer. Cover with aluminum foil and pie weights (dried beans work well), and place on the preheated baking sheet. Bake for 12 minutes. Remove from oven and take out weights and foil. Lower heat to 350 degrees and bake an additional 10 to 18 minutes, depending on whether you want the crust partially or fully baked. For the yogurt tart, you will need a fully baked crust.

leeks

celeriac

pumpkins

November

apples

November

FEATURED
INGREDIENTS

Apples,
Celeriac,
Leeks,
Pumpkin

BY NOW, THE HARVEST IS NEARLY OVER. Kale, the hardy and nutritious friend of the cool-weather gardener, is still available. Other greens, even lettuce, may also hang on, depending on your location and the temperature. But the ground is no longer yielding much. If you're lucky, you have a greenhouse nearby to help out.

Many farmer's markets continue until Thanksgiving, although the variety of produce has diminished. Many root crops, cabbages, and winter squashes—items that remain tasty after weeks or even months under proper care—are here in big supply. You'll also find apples and cranberries to brighten the market table and the menu.

Consider yourself lucky, too, if your town has an indoor farmer's market, or if you can, sign up for a winter CSA (community supported agriculture) share. Our winter CSA comes from Wolf Pine Farm in southern Maine. It coordinates with other farms in the area to provide not just potatoes, parsnips, and carrots, but also honey, oats, frozen blueberries, and other treats to liven up the long winter in the kitchen.

The culinary highlight of November, of course, is Thanksgiving. The holiday is a perfect showcase for local produce, as many traditional side dishes and desserts involve our region's best-known seasonal items, including squash, cranberries, and pumpkin. One way to update your spread is to cook some of the lesser-known root vegetables, such as celeriac and rutabaga, for your Thanksgiving table.

Dutch Baby (Apple Pancake)

There are many versions of this pancake. Some people like to cook the apples up separately as a topping, but I like mine right in the pancake. As for what makes this "Dutch" or "baby," I have no idea.

SERVES **4**

2 eggs

2/3 cup whole milk

1/2 tsp vanilla

pinch salt

1/2 cup flour

2 small apples, peeled, cored, and cut into 1/4-inch slices

1 Tbsp butter

1 Tbsp sugar mixed with 1/2 tsp cinnamon

powdered sugar, for serving

lemon wedges or cheddar cheese for serving

Preheat oven to 425 degrees.

In a large bowl, whisk eggs, milk, vanilla, and salt. Beat well, by hand or in a blender, until thick and foamy. Add flour and beat well to combine. Stir in the apple slices.

Place a 9-inch cake pan (not a springform pan) in the hot oven for several minutes. Remove and place butter in pan, swirling to melt it and to coat bottom of pan. Scrape pancake batter into pan and sprinkle with cinnamon-sugar mixture. Bake for 20 minutes, until puffy and browning on the edges. Reduce heat to 375 degrees and cook for an additional 10 minutes, until nicely browned.

Sprinkle pancake with powdered sugar and serve with lemon wedges (to squeeze over the pancake) or with cubes of cheddar cheese. Best eaten right away.

Apples

Who can say which is better: a handful of plump strawberries, a juicy peach, or a perfectly ripe cantaloupe? They all sound pretty tempting. Nonetheless, I think a strong case could be made for the apple as top-ranking fruit. Apples are delicious both raw and cooked. They are the perfect handheld snack, great when sliced into salads, and convenient to add to lunchboxes. Nutritionally, apples don't offer as much as blueberries or oranges, but they do have some vitamin C and a lot of fiber. When I was in school a friend once asked me whether I was on a special diet. Every time he saw me, I was eating an apple. I pointed out that it was apple season, and any intelligent person would be eating as many fresh apples as possible. Although apples store well, if you want that first bite to really crunch, only just-picked will do.

Applesauce Two Ways

I like a lazy method of making applesauce. To eliminate peeling, coring, and chopping the apples, I roast them and use a food mill to separate the unwanted parts. As long as you bake the fruit long enough to get it really soft, using the food mill is easy. Plus, roasting gives the sauce a slightly caramelized taste. The stovetop method, which follows, works great, too.

MAKES **4** CUPS

1 1/2 lbs apples, washed

1 to 4 Tbsp brown sugar or maple syrup, if you want sweetening

pinch of salt

1 Tbsp lemon juice

1/4 cup water or apple cider

1/2 tsp cinnamon

1/2 tsp vanilla

For applesauce from roasted apples

Preheat oven to 400 degrees. Halve apples and place in 9 x 13-inch baking pan. Sprinkle with brown sugar or maple syrup, salt, and lemon juice. Pour 1/4 cup water or apple cider over the apples. Roast them in the oven for 40 minutes, or more if needed, until apples are so soft they are splitting and exploding. Cool the fruit, then pass through a food mill to separate peels and seeds from the puree. Stir in cinnamon and vanilla. It's good eaten warm or cold.

For stovetop applesauce

Peel the apples or not, whichever you prefer. Core the apples, and cut them into 1/4-inch pieces. Place in a large saucepan with sugar, salt, lemon juice, and cinnamon. Add water to barely cover the bottom of the pan. Bring to a boil over medium-high heat, then lower heat to medium-low, and simmer, partly covered, stirring regularly, until apple chunks lose their shape, about 15 minutes. Remove from heat and add vanilla. Mash with a potato masher for chunkier sauce, or whirl in a food processor for smoother sauce. You can also pass it through a food mill to remove apple peels.

APPLESAUCE BASICS

Applesauce must be made according to a household's preferences: sweetened or not, chunky or smooth, spiced or plain, peeled or not. Applesauce made with unpeeled apples is pink, and (to me) a bit more flavorful. But you'll either need to use a hand-cranked food mill to get the peels out, or have a family that doesn't mind bits of peel in their sauce. Whichever you prefer, be sure to include at least a pinch of salt and a sprinkle of lemon juice. Both highlight the apple flavor, and their lack is noticeable if left out.

Veiled Peasant Girls

The movies of Ingmar Bergman have shown that Scandinavians have unexpected emotional depths. The name of this delicious, no-bake dessert confirms it. Don't expect the bread crumbs to stay crisp when surrounded by all that applesauce and cream; they're still tasty even when they get a bit soggy.

SERVES **8**

2 Tbsp butter

1 1/2 5-oz packages melba toasts, crushed into crumbs (or substitute 3 cups homemade bread crumbs; commercial bread crumbs will have an unpleasant texture)

1/4 cup sugar, divided

1 tsp cinnamon

1/2 tsp cardamom

1/4 tsp nutmeg

2 cups heavy cream

1 tsp vanilla

4 1/2 cups applesauce

1 Tbsp brandy (optional)

Melt butter in a large saucepan over medium heat. Add crumbs, 3 tablespoons sugar, and spices. Stir to combine. Cook, stirring frequently, until fragrant and browned, 4 or 5 minutes. Remove from heat and let cool. Reserve 2 tablespoons of the crumbs and set aside.

Add the vanilla and the remaining sugar to the heavy cream and whip until it forms medium-stiff peaks. Stir brandy into the applesauce.

Sprinkle one-third of the crumbs (about 2/3 cup) in the bottom of a serving bowl. A glass dish is nice if you have it, or prepare these in individual dessert dishes or glasses for maximum visual appeal.

Dollop 1 1/2 cups of applesauce all over the crumbs, then smooth gently into an even layer. The crumbs will want to stick to the applesauce, but do your best. Top the applesauce with one-third of the whipped cream and spread into an even layer. Repeat layers, ending with a layer of whipped cream. Sprinkle top with reserved crumbs. You may serve it right away, or let chill for a couple of hours before eating.

Pork Chops and Apples with Celeriac

You'll need thick pork chops; thin ones just won't work. Fortunately, thick pork chops are usually available at farmer's markets.

SERVES **4**

1 cup very hot water

3 Tbsp plus 1/2 tsp salt, divided

2 Tbsp brown sugar

3 cups cold water

2 lbs thick-cut pork chops (2 to 4 chops, depending on their size)

1 bulb celeriac

4 cloves garlic

1/2 tsp dried thyme

1/2 tsp black pepper

3 Tbsp apple cider vinegar

1/4 cup apple cider or other juice

2 Tbsp maple syrup

1 Tbsp butter

1 Tbsp olive oil

2 large or 3 medium apples, peeled, cored, and cut into rough 2-inch chunks

Preheat the oven to 350 degrees.

Pour the hot water into a medium mixing bowl. Add 3 tablespoons salt and the sugar and stir until mostly dissolved. Pour in the cold water and then add the pork chops, submerging them in the brine. Let them sit while you prepare the other components of the dish.

Peel the celeriac and cut into small cubes, about 1/2-inch thick. Peel the garlic cloves and slice them thinly. Put the garlic in a small dish with the thyme, 1/2 teaspoon salt, and black pepper. Mix vinegar, cider, and maple syrup in a small measuring cup. Add the butter to the cup (it won't mix in; that's okay).

Choose a roasting pan which can hold all the chops without overlap, and place pan in the oven to warm up. (This will also be your serving dish.)

Heat the olive oil in a large skillet over medium-high heat. Remove the chops from their water bath, pat them dry with paper towels, and place in the skillet. Cook undisturbed for 3 minutes each side, until well browned. Remove the skillet from the heat, and move the chops to the preheated roasting pan in the oven. Roast until chops are mostly done (about 145 degrees on an instant-read thermometer). This will take about 4 minutes, but the exact time will depend on the thickness of the chops. When chops are done, remove them from the oven and cover the roasting pan with aluminum foil while they rest.

Meanwhile, replace the skillet on the burner and turn to medium heat. Add celeriac and cook, stirring every so often, until it starts to brown on all sides, about 6 minutes. (If celeriac sticks, add a teaspoon or two of olive oil.) Add the garlic/thyme mixture and the apples to the pan and cook, stirring constantly, for 1 to 2 minutes, until mixture is very fragrant and garlic is turning golden. Add the cider mixture to the pan and turn burner to medium-low. Scrape the bottom of the pan to incorporate any browned bits, and bring to a rolling boil. Simmer sauce for 6 to 8 minutes, until sauce has thickened and apples have softened but not fallen apart. Pour the apples, celeriac, and sauce over the rested chops, and serve.

Roasted Celeriac and Potatoes

Celeriac is fine roasted on its own, but I like to give it some company. Sweet potatoes are nice here, too, either added in or as a substitute for the regular potatoes.

SERVES **4** TO **6** AS A SIDE DISH

1 1/2 lbs celeriac, peeled and cut into 1-inch chunks

1 1/2 lbs potatoes, peeled and cut into 2-inch chunks

1 tsp dried thyme

3 Tbsp olive oil

1 tsp salt

6 cloves garlic, peeled

black pepper

Preheat oven to 425 degrees. Place celeriac and potatoes on a rimmed baking sheet. Sprinkle with thyme, and drizzle with olive oil. Toss to coat. Sprinkle with salt and roast in the oven for 20 minutes. Remove, add the garlic cloves, stir, and roast for another 15 to 20 minutes, until vegetables are nicely browned. Adjust seasonings to taste.

Celeriac

Poor celeriac—brown, lumpy, craggy—is not easy on the eyes. But in the vegetable world, it's best not to judge by appearances. After all, those supermarket tomatoes certainly look beautifully ripe, but inside they conceal a mealy disappointment. How much more pleasant to pick up the homely celeriac and discover that it's a tasty treat. Celeriac is a variety of celery bred to have a large starchy root instead of fibrous crunchy stalks. Celeriac tastes something like celery with a kind of herbal overtone. It can be sliced and enjoyed in its crunchy, raw state; combined with other root vegetables in purees and stews; or cut into batons to fry, making a healthier version of French fries. Just make sure to peel away that lumpy skin first.

Winter Waldorf

In France, grated celeriac with a creamy dressing, céleri rémoulade, *is a favorite preparation. Because of celeriac's flavor, similar to regular celery, this dish reminds me of a Waldorf salad. If you want to simplify the recipe, leave out the apples and walnuts and use less dressing, and enjoy the grated celeriac as a slaw.*

SERVES **6** AS A SIDE SALAD

1/2 cup chopped walnuts

2 medium bulbs of celeriac, peeled and grated

2 Tbsp minced shallots

1 small apple, cored and chopped

2 Tbsp lemon juice

3 Tbsp mayonnaise

2 Tbsp sour cream or crème fraîche

1 Tbsp Dijon mustard

1/2 tsp salt

1/4 tsp pepper

1 Tbsp minced parsley or chives (optional)

Preheat oven to 350 degrees. Place nuts on a baking sheet and toast for 6 to 8 minutes, until fragrant. Let cool.

Put celeriac, shallots, and apple in a medium serving dish and drizzle with lemon juice. Toss to coat. In a small bowl, whisk together mayonnaise, sour cream, mustard, salt, and pepper to make the dressing. Add walnuts to the celeriac/apple mixture. Spoon dressing over the mixture and fold it in to combine. Serve with minced herbs sprinkled on top.

STORING WINTER VEGETABLES

There are few places in the average modern home or apartment which will give you the ideal conditions for most winter-storage vegetables. Most need a temperature between freezing and 40 degrees, which a refrigerator can provide, but they also need a very high degree of humidity—far above what a refrigerator offers. And then there are some crops which need somewhat less humidity, and some that need somewhat higher temperatures. Generally, your farmer is going to do a better job storing vegetables over the long haul than you can as an individual. My view is that it doesn't pay to stock up on storage crops. If you really want to create your own root cellar, check the **Resources** section (page 175) for sources and places to get advice.

I keep all my winter vegetables in the refrigerator, except for garlic, squash, and pumpkins, and I try to use them quickly. Potato experts frown upon storing potatoes in the refrigerator, as they can become too sweet, but if you keep them in a cabinet, the warm temperature can cause them to soften, and on the counter they can turn green and sprout. The best thing to do is to buy winter vegetables in small quantities, and eat them regularly!

Cauliflower and Leek Soup

Feel free to vary the seasonings here. I like nutmeg in creamy soups, but curry is good, too, and also gives the soup a nice color.

SERVES **6**

1 Tbsp olive oil

1 Tbsp butter

4 to 6 leeks, cleaned and sliced 1/4-inch thick, using white and light-green part only

1 tsp salt

2 garlic cloves, smashed

1 small head cauliflower or 1/2 large head, cut into small florets

1/2 cup white wine or vermouth

4 1/2 cups vegetable or chicken broth

1 medium potato, cut into 1/2-inch dice

1/4 tsp nutmeg (or substitute 1 to 2 tsp curry powder)

1/2 cup heavy cream

1 to 2 Tbsp sherry

salt and white pepper

minced chives or parsley for serving

In a large pot, heat oil and butter over medium heat. When foaming subsides, add the leeks and salt. Cook, stirring occasionally, until leeks soften and begin to brown, about 6 minutes. Add garlic to pot and cook, stirring, for 30 seconds. Add cauliflower florets and cook, stirring often, for about 3 minutes, to begin softening cauliflower. Add wine. Cook, stirring occasionally, until liquid is mostly evaporated.

Add broth and potato and bring to a boil. Lower to a simmer and cook until cauliflower and potato are tender, about 10 minutes.

If desired, remove a ladleful of florets and potato cubes to add back into the soup at serving. Puree remainder of soup with an immersion blender or in a stand-up blender. Return soup to pot and add nutmeg, cream, sherry, and any reserved florets or potato. Adjust seasoning with salt and white pepper. Sprinkle each serving with minced herbs.

Leeks

Leeks are in the onion family, but are milder and dirtier. Their tightly bound leaves can collect a lot of soil in between their layers, making it essential to wash them thoroughly before using. You can cut them into lengths and soak them, or cut them in half and rinse them in a colander. When cooking with leeks, use the white and light-green part of the stalks. The green part, too tough to eat, can be used for flavoring stocks and then discarded. Leeks go well with potatoes, fish, cauliflower—any food where you want some onion flavor, but not an overpowering one. I suppose it goes without saying that leeks are a favorite of Norwegian cooks.

Leek and Potato Frittata

I often have trouble removing a frittata from the pan, so sometimes I just serve portions directly from the skillet. I have included instructions on removal, if you want to try. Two leeks may seem like too many for this dish, but they will cook down.

SERVES **4** AS A SMALL MAIN COURSE

7 eggs

3 Tbsp creamy goat cheese (about 2 oz)

1/4 tsp salt

1/4 tsp pepper

2 slices bacon, diced

2 medium potatoes, peeled and sliced 1/4-inch thick

2 Tbsp water

2 leeks, cleaned and sliced 1/4-inch thick, white and light green parts only

1/2 cup grated Gruyère or other cheese

In a large measuring cup, use a fork to beat together eggs, goat cheese, salt, and pepper. The goat cheese will remain in chunks; just try to make sure they aren't too large.

Put bacon and potato slices in an ovenproof 8- or 9-inch skillet with 2 tablespoons of water. Heat to medium. Bring to a boil and allow water to cook off, stirring regularly. After water has evaporated, continue cooking for 4 or 5 minutes, still stirring occasionally, letting bacon fat render and potatoes brown a bit. Add leeks and cook, stirring often, until significantly cooked down, about 5 more minutes.

Preheat broiler, to low setting (if you have one). Reduce the skillet's heat to medium-low and pour in egg mixture. Cook eggs on stovetop, without stirring, until mostly set. If you poke a knife into the frittata, you don't want a lot of egg running out, but don't let it get bone-dry, either. It will take about 5 or 6 minutes to get to this point. Scatter grated cheese on top of the eggs, then put skillet under broiler for 1 to 3 minutes, depending on your broiler's heat, until the frittata is cooked through and browned a bit on top.

To remove from the pan, run a sharp knife around the edges. Take a flexible metal spatula and slide it as far under the frittata as you can to loosen it from the bottom. Place serving plate on top of skillet and flip skillet over. If pieces remain stuck to the pan, scrape them off carefully and replace them on the frittata.

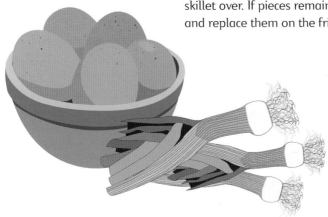

Mormor's Fish Soup with Leeks

Mormor *means "maternal grandmother" in Norwegian. My kids call my mother Mormor, although their cousins call her Farmor (paternal grandmother), which can get confusing. The mormor in this recipe refers to* my *mormor, Petra, who still fished the Oslo fjords for whiting into her eighties. The woman appreciated fresh fish.*

SERVES **4**

1 quart fish broth (see recipe)

2 large or 3 medium leeks, cleaned and thinly sliced (white and light-green parts only)

2 medium carrots, sliced into 1/4-inch-thick coins

2 egg yolks

1 cup half-and-half

1 1/2 lbs thick haddock fillets, cut into 1 1/2-inch chunks

salt and white pepper

For fish broth
1 quart water

2 fish-broth bouillon cubes

1/2 medium onion, sliced

1 bay leaf

1 carrot, halved

3 sprigs dill

pinch of sugar

1 Tbsp white vinegar

Bring broth to a boil in a medium saucepan and reduce to a gentle simmer. Add leeks and carrots. Simmer until tender, about 15 minutes. While soup is simmering, whisk egg yolks and half-and-half together in a medium bowl or measuring cup.

When vegetables are tender, add fish chunks to broth. Simmer until cooked, which will only take 2 or 3 minutes. Remove pot from heat. Slowly pour two ladlefuls of hot soup into the egg yolk mixture, whisking briskly the whole time. The whisking is essential or the eggs will scramble. Pour this mixture back into the soup pot, again whisking the whole time. Season with salt and white pepper. You may heat the soup over low heat to bring back to serving temperature, but do not boil it.

Fish broth
Many fish markets sell fish broth they make themselves, which is an easy way to get a good base for this dish. You can make your own broth from scratch, but you'll need fish parts (bones especially) and about an hour. Or you can cheat and use this recipe. It comes directly from a Norwegian, so it can't be that bad. The same Norwegian stresses that you should not substitute clam broth, because the clam flavor is too strong.

Bring the water and bouillon to boil. Add remaining ingredients. Simmer for 10 minutes, then strain and use the broth in the soup recipe (above).

Pumpkin Pie

The technique for this pie comes from the Cooking for Engineers website—or at least, that's where I first saw it. The proportions and seasoning are my own.

SERVES **8**

1 9-inch pie shell, prebaked (see **Raspberry Yogurt Tart** on page 27)

1 1/4 cups pumpkin puree (canned or homemade; see recipe on page 41)

2/3 cup light brown sugar

2 Tbsp sugar

3/4 tsp ginger

3/4 tsp cinnamon

1/4 tsp mace (or substitute nutmeg)

1/4 tsp allspice

1/2 tsp salt

1/2 cup heavy cream

1/3 cup milk

2 eggs

1 egg yolk

2 tsp bourbon

1/2 tsp vanilla

Place a rimmed baking sheet in oven and turn heat to 375 degrees.

Cook pumpkin, sugars, spices, and salt in a medium saucepan over medium heat. When mixture is hot all the way through, stir in cream and milk. Mix thoroughly, and continue to stir while heating. Cook until bubbling, then remove from heat and transfer to a large measuring cup with a pouring spout (unless your saucepan has a spout).

Put eggs and egg yolk in a blender and whirl briefly to combine. Turn blender on steady, and slowly pour in hot pumpkin mixture. When completely blended, add bourbon and vanilla.

Pour into prebaked pie shell, place on preheated baking sheet, and bake the pie for 25 to 30 minutes. The filling should shake like jelly when done. Do not overbake it. Let pie cool for at least 1 hour before cutting. Serve with whipped cream.

Pumpkin

Pumpkin is not the same as winter squash—close, but not the same. Most of us only eat pumpkin in pie or sweet bread, and as a result, most of us think pumpkin tastes like allspice and cinnamon. Actually, pumpkin tastes like a denser, heartier type of squash. It stands up well to many different preparations, especially baking and roasting. Keep in mind that the big pumpkins at farmer's markets are strictly decorative. Eat those and you will end up with a very stringy mouthful. The pumpkins to cook are the small ones, sometimes called pie pumpkins or sugar pumpkins.

Pumpkin Lasagne

Making pumpkin puree from scratch is a time commitment. Even though it's easy to do, it's an extra step that not everyone feels like taking. The good news is that roasting the pumpkin saves you from peeling it. The other good news is that you can make a whole bunch of puree at once and freeze leftovers in small amounts, so that next time you need some, it's ready to go.

SERVES **8** TO **10**

1/4 cup white wine or vermouth

2 cloves garlic

1/2 tsp thyme

salt

2 cups ricotta cheese

1/2 cup soft goat cheese (4 oz)

3/4 cup grated Parmesan cheese, divided

1 cup half-and-half or whole milk, divided

1/4 cup minced parsley

1/4 tsp chili powder (or more to taste)

pepper

3 cups pumpkin puree (see recipe on page 41; if using canned, this will be about 2 cans)

1/4 tsp nutmeg

15 no-boil lasagne noodles

1 cup shredded fontina cheese

Bring wine, garlic, thyme, and 1/2 teaspoon salt to a simmer in a small saucepan. Simmer until liquid is reduced by half. Remove from heat.

In a medium bowl, combine ricotta, goat cheese, 1/2 cup of the Parmesan, 1/2 cup of the half-and-half or milk, parsley, and chili powder. Season with salt and pepper.

In another bowl, combine pumpkin puree and remaining half-and-half. Stir in the wine mixture and season with salt, pepper, and nutmeg.

Preheat oven to 400 degrees. In a 9 x 13-inch baking dish, spread 3/4 cup pumpkin mixture. Top with three lasagne noodles. Do not overlap noodles, or even let them touch; they need to absorb moisture to cook, and all sides need to be exposed to sauce to allow that to happen. Spread 1/3 cup ricotta mixture over each noodle (1 cup per layer). Place three noodles on top. Spread 1/2 cup pumpkin mixture on top of each noodle (1 1/2 cups per layer). Repeat layering, ending with a layer of noodles covered with ricotta. Top with fontina and remaining 1/4 cup of Parmesan. Cover pan with foil and bake 25 minutes. Remove foil and bake an additional 10 to 15 minutes, until browned and bubbling. Let sit 5 minutes before serving.

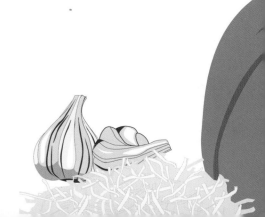

For pumpkin puree

2 cooking pumpkins (or more, if you want extra), halved, seeds removed, and each half cut into 4 wedges

1 tsp salt

Pumpkin puree

Preheat oven to 400 degrees. On an oiled, rimmed baking sheet, place pumpkin wedges skin side down and sprinkle with salt. Roast until tender, anywhere from 30 to 60 minutes, depending on the thickness of the pumpkin flesh. When done, the pumpkin should be collapsing. Cool pumpkin enough to handle, then scrape flesh into the bowl of a food processor. Process it until smooth. Set aside three cups of puree for the lasagne.

To freeze the remainder, assess how watery your puree is. Many cooking pumpkins are not watery at all, but it's good to check. To remove excess water, spread puree out over several layers of paper towels and let sit for 15 minutes. Remove, portion, and seal in containers, Ziploc bags, or ice cube trays to freeze.

ROASTING PUMPKIN SEEDS

Roasting pumpkin seeds is a great side pleasure of eating real pumpkins (or carving a jack-o'-lantern). The hardest part is separating the seeds themselves from the stringy innards. Once that's done, you just spread them out on a sheet pan, mix them with some oil or melted butter, salt, and other seasonings if you like, and roast in a 350-degree oven. It helps to stir them every so often and to check on how they are browning. I find that 20 or 30 minutes is enough for me; some people like them much darker.

Cheesy Stuffed Roasted Pumpkin

A few years ago this delicious recipe went viral. It's an old favorite from the wonderful Ruth Reichl, former Gourmet *magazine editor, who mentioned it during an interview on National Public Radio in 2009. From there it was tweeted, blogged about, tested, and eaten all over the place, including at our house. You can easily find the original version online; this is just a variation. Reichl specifies using a baguette, but I have used other types of bread, including whole-grain, and it always tastes delicious. Note that the bread filling should be quite strongly seasoned, because the pumpkin flesh itself is not.*

SERVES 4 TO 6 AS A MAIN DISH

6 cups of 1 1/2-inch bread cubes, cut from any kind of sturdy bread

2 small (5 to 6 inches in diameter) sugar pumpkins, or one larger one

salt and pepper

1/2 cup white wine

1 3/4 cups vegetable or chicken broth

3/4 cup heavy cream

1 garlic clove, minced

1/2 tsp nutmeg

white pepper

1 cup shredded fontina cheese (about 4 oz)

1 cup shredded Emmentaler cheese (or other Swiss cheese) (about 4 oz)

1/4 cup grated Parmesan cheese (about 1/2 oz)

cooking oil for brushing pumpkin (optional)

Preheat oven to 425 degrees. Spread bread cubes on a sheet tray and toast them in the oven until crisped, about 10 minutes. Let cool.

Prepare a rimmed sheet pan by lining it with foil and lightly oiling the foil. Cut off the top of the pumpkins about 2 inches from the top. You need to make an opening large enough to easily scrape out and stuff the pumpkin. Save the top. Using a large spoon, scrape out all the seeds and as many of the stringy bits as possible from the pumpkin, making sure to leave a sturdy bottom. Season the inside with salt and pepper. If you want, save the seeds for roasting later (see **Roasting Pumpkin Seeds** tip on page 41).

Whisk wine, broth, cream, garlic, nutmeg, white pepper, and 1/2 teaspoon salt in a measuring cup. Mix cheeses together in a separate bowl.

Place pumpkins on the prepared baking sheet. Put a layer of bread cubes in the bottom of the pumpkin, and top with a layer of cheese mixture. Continue layering until pumpkin is filled to within a half-inch of the opening. Pour broth mixture over layers, giving it time to seep into all the spaces. You may have some bread, cheese, and/or broth left over. Resist the urge to overstuff the pumpkin, as the filling will puff up while baking.

Replace the pumpkin top and brush the outside of the pumpkin with oil. (You won't be eating the outside, but the oil will help the skin brown and look prettier, if that is important to you.) Bake for 30 minutes at 425 degrees. Reduce heat to 350 degrees and bake until pumpkin is soft but not collapsed, about another hour. Bring them to the table still whole, and scoop out some of the pumpkin flesh with each serving.

December

oats

cranberries

winter squash

garlic

December

FEATURED
INGREDIENTS

**Cranberries,
Garlic,
Oats,
Winter Squash**

COLD, SHORT DAYS are upon us. In Caribou, Maine, on the Canadian border, residents will enjoy less than eight hours of daylight. Greenwich, Connecticut, the southernmost town in New England, will only have half an hour more. The darker afternoons and colder air make us long for comfort foods and increase our desire to use the oven to bake breads and sweets.

Most people celebrate a holiday in December that involves plenty of cooking—Christmas, Hanukkah, Kwanzaa, New Year's Eve. And even if you keep your home celebrations simple, chances are your workplace or your kid's school will be asking for cookies, a casserole, or some kind of festive appetizer.

Dessert is a good place to feature local treats. Forget the bûche de Noël and make a dessert using frozen cranberries or blueberries, or perhaps applesauce. Carrot cupcakes will thrill most anyone, and with local carrots in them, what could be better?

You might feel like you don't have a lot of time and energy for everyday meals. Fortunately, you can easily enhance a meal by roasting some of the local root vegetables (parsnips, potatoes, celeriac) readily available at this time of year. They also shine in soups and stews. What could be more comforting than a warm bowl of soup or a plate of delicious caramelized vegetables at the end of a dark, cold day?

Chicken with Tangy Cranberry Sauce

Serve this chicken with something to sop up the sauce, such as plain rice, good bread, or mashed potatoes. This dish also goes well with stuffing.

SERVES **4** TO **6**

2 lbs bone-in chicken thighs

salt and pepper

2 Tbsp canola oil

1 small onion, chopped into small pieces

1 celery rib, chopped into small pieces

2 cloves garlic, minced or pressed

2 Tbsp tomato paste

1 1/2 cups cranberries, fresh or frozen

1/3 cup maple syrup

1 Tbsp whole-grain mustard

1 tsp paprika

1/2 tsp chili powder

Pat chicken dry with paper towels. Season with salt and pepper and set into a 9 x 13-inch baking pan, skin side up. Preheat oven to 375 degrees.

In a medium skillet, heat oil over medium heat. Add onion, celery, and 1/2 teaspoon salt. Sauté until softened, about 5 minutes. Add garlic and cook, stirring, until fragrant, about 30 seconds. Add tomato paste and cook 2 minutes, stirring constantly. Add cranberries, maple syrup, and mustard. Stir well, scraping up any bits from the bottom of the pan. Stir in paprika, chili powder, and 1/2 teaspoon pepper. Bring to a boil, then reduce heat and simmer, uncovered, until the sauce thickens and cranberries have begun to burst, about 6 to 8 minutes.

Pat chicken dry once more with paper towel. Pour cranberry sauce around chicken and bake 30 minutes, until nearly done (when interior at thickest part of thigh registers about 160 degrees on a meat thermometer). Remove pan from oven and change oven setting to broil. Baste chicken pieces with a small amount of sauce, and broil until sauce is bubbling, anywhere from 1 to 3 minutes.

Cranberries

These sour berries are native to North America yet undervalued here. I think if they were native to France, there would be dozens of sublime pastries and sauces starring the fruit. Instead, we cook them with sugar for relish, or dry them and throw them into muffins. Cranberries have a lot more potential than that. Their tartness makes an excellent foil to overly sweet holiday desserts. They freeze easily; just throw a bag of fresh cranberries right into the freezer, and they'll be ready whenever you want them. Their sparkling color makes them festive, perfect for a holiday spread.

Cranberry Blueberry Shortbread Bars

Here's a colorful way to end a winter meal. Like most bars, these freeze well. If you double the recipe, use a 9 x 13-inch pan, and freeze half the bars. If you are doubling, you can use a whole egg instead of two yolks, if it's easier.

MAKES **16** SMALL SQUARES

10 Tbsp butter

1 cup sugar, divided

1/2 tsp salt

1/2 tsp ginger

pinch nutmeg

1 tsp lemon zest

1 egg yolk

1 tsp vanilla

1 1/2 tsp brandy

2 cups flour

1 cup cranberries, fresh or frozen

1 Tbsp lemon juice

1 Tbsp water

1/2 cup blueberries, fresh or frozen

3 Tbsp brown sugar

Grease an 8 x 8-inch baking pan and line with parchment paper.

Melt butter in a medium saucepan over low heat. When melted, remove from heat and stir in 1/3 cup sugar, salt, ginger, nutmeg, and zest, mixing well. Stir in egg yolk, vanilla, and brandy and mix thoroughly. Stir in flour to make a stiff dough. Set aside 2/3 cup of the dough in a small bowl. Press the remaining larger portion of dough into the bottom of the pan, covering it. Prick dough a dozen times with a fork and chill in the refrigerator.

Preheat oven to 325 degrees. When oven is ready, bake crust for 18 minutes, until it looks dry.

Meanwhile, make the filling and the topping. Bring cranberries, remaining 2/3 cup sugar, lemon juice, and water to a boil. Reduce heat and simmer 5 minutes. Add blueberries and simmer an additional 2 minutes. Remove from heat and let rest until crust is baked.

With your fingers, mix the brown sugar in with the set-aside dough.

When shortbread crust has baked, remove from oven and raise heat to 350 degrees. Pour berry mixture over warm crust. Scatter remaining dough on top in small clumps. Bake 35 minutes, until topping appears light brown and crunchy. Cool completely or chill before cutting.

Spiced Cranberry Relish

I've never loved either traditional cranberry sauce or completely raw cranberry relishes. This recipe is my compromise. It's very tasty and a bit runny. Use it as an accompaniment to meals year-round, not just at Thanksgiving. It's great with cheese or ham, or even as a topping for yogurt or vanilla ice cream.

MAKES **1** CUP

1 cup whole cranberries, fresh or frozen, divided

6 Tbsp sugar, divided

1 Tbsp lemon or orange juice

Pinch grated orange or lemon zest

1/2 tsp chopped fresh ginger

1/4 tsp cardamom (optional)

1/4 tsp cinnamon

pinch ground cloves

1/4 tsp salt

pinch white pepper

Put half the cranberries in a small pot with 4 tablespoons sugar and the juice and zest. Cook over medium heat until sugar is dissolved and berries have burst, about 10 to 15 minutes. Remove from heat.

Put remaining half of cranberries, remaining sugar, all spices, and salt and white pepper into the bowl of a small food processor. Pulse until chopped medium-fine, about eight pulses. Combine in a bowl with the cooked cranberries, and let sit at least 30 minutes for flavors to mingle.

Cranberry Punch

Punch is underutilized. It's festive, and everyone is always happy to see it at a party. Plus, you can leave the alcohol on the side and let grown-ups fix their glasses to their own taste. This punch does include bits of cranberries; if your audience is very fussy about such things, you might want to strain them out.

MAKES **1 1/2** QUARTS (without alcohol)

3 cups cranberries, fresh or frozen

1 cup sugar

2 Tbsp water

1/2 tsp cinnamon

1 cup orange juice

2 cups cranberry blend juice

3 lemons (2 juiced, 1 with ends trimmed and sliced)

2 oranges, ends trimmed and sliced

1 cinnamon stick

1 quart seltzer

3 oz dark rum

3 oz vodka

1 oz Cointreau

Put the cranberries, sugar, water, and cinnamon in a medium saucepan. Heat over medium-high heat until bubbling. Using a potato masher or wooden spoon, smash the berries until most of the cranberries have burst and the sugar is dissolving. Remove from heat. Stir in orange juice, cranberry juice, and the juice from two lemons. Add cinnamon stick. Chill for several hours to allow flavors to meld.

To serve, pour punch into a bowl or pitcher (straining it, if need be) and gently pour in seltzer. Add orange and lemon slices to float on top. Add spirits directly to bowl, or combine and keep separate in a small pitcher. Serve ice on the side to keep it from diluting the punch.

SMOOTHIES

Frozen fruit smoothies are a great way to have local fruit during a New England winter. The basic components of a smoothie allow for infinite variants. For four 8-ounce smoothies, blend 2 cups of frozen berries, 1 3/4 cups liquid (juice, milk, yogurt, buttermilk, or a combination), and a sweetener, if you choose. A little honey and/or lemon juice are good additions, as is a ripe banana. You can add more frozen fruit if you'd like it fruitier or thicker. And don't forget that cranberries count as fruit, too.

Spaghetti with Garlic and Parsley

As graduate students, my father and his housemates took turns making lunch. Someone figured out that bologna sandwiches were the quickest and cheapest way to serve lunch to a crowd, and that's what they ended up eating for an entire year. If the students had been in Italy, this might be the dish they reverted to. Spaghetti with garlic is simple, quick, and cheap. Everyone's variation is a bit different. Use more or less garlic, more or less parsley—really, more or less of anything.

SERVES **4**

5 Tbsp extra virgin olive oil, divided

3 or 4 thick slices of bread, crumbled or processed to make 1 generous cup of bread crumbs

8 cloves garlic, peeled and sliced

salt and pepper

12 oz spaghetti

1 1/2 cups coarsely chopped Italian parsley

1/2 cup grated Parmesan cheese

Heat 1 tablespoon of olive oil and the bread crumbs with a pinch of salt in a medium skillet over medium heat. Stir regularly and keep cooking until bread crumbs are dry and lightly browned, about 5 minutes. Set aside.

Heat the remaining oil, garlic, 1/2 teaspoon salt, and 1/4 teaspoon pepper in small skillet over medium-low heat. Keep an eye on the garlic and stir it regularly, so it does not brown. When garlic turns golden, remove skillet from heat.

Meanwhile, cook spaghetti, reserving a cup of pasta water. Drain spaghetti and turn into a large serving bowl. Add garlic with all its oil, the parsley, and 2 tablespoons of pasta water. Toss repeatedly, to combine well and to let the heat of the pasta wilt the parsley. If pasta seems dry, add another spoonful of pasta water. Add the toasted bread crumbs and the Parmesan, and salt and pepper to taste. Serve with additional cheese.

Garlic

There's a Norwegian saying: "If you are missing salt, you are missing everything." This is true enough in cooking. Norwegians traditionally do not use much garlic, so I don't know that they would agree with my addendum: "If you are missing garlic, you are also missing everything." But that's pretty apt for many of us, and is probably one reason why Italian cuisine is more popular than Norwegian (sorry, Mamma). Garlic is a vital component of so many sauces and marinades. Even with a good harvest and a generous farm share, it's hard to ever have too much garlic. But just in case that ever happens to you, here are a couple of recipes which use a lot of it.

Leftover Turkey with Garlicky "Mole" Sauce

This sauce is not authentic; it's a stripped-down, speedy version, good for holiday leftovers. The spiciness level is suitable for those born and raised in New England. If you increase the chipotles, or add other chiles, increase the garlic too, or you won't taste much of it. This recipe makes 2 cups of sauce, and can easily be doubled. The sauce freezes well.

SERVES **4**

1/4 cup raisins or chopped prunes

1/4 cup sliced or slivered almonds

6 cloves garlic, peeled and left whole

1 Tbsp sesame seeds

1/2 small or medium onion, chopped

3/4 cup diced tomatoes, canned or fresh, with their juice

1 small chipotle pepper with 1 tsp adobo sauce from can (or more to taste)

1/2 corn tortilla, torn into pieces, or 5 or 6 tortilla chips

1 tsp dried oregano

1/2 tsp cinnamon

1/4 tsp coriander

1/4 tsp ground cloves

1/2 tsp salt

1 Tbsp corn or canola oil

1 oz unsweetened chocolate, chopped

1/2 cup chicken broth or water

3 cups turkey meat, shredded or roughly chopped

Place raisins in small (non-plastic) bowl and add boiling water just to cover. Leave to rehydrate.

Toast almonds and garlic in a dry skillet over medium heat for 5 minutes. Add sesame seeds and toast 2 more minutes. The mixture should become fragrant but not deeply browned. Transfer to a blender. Add raisins and their water, onion, tomatoes and juice, chipotle and adobo sauce, tortilla, remaining spices, and salt. Puree until smooth.

Heat oil in a medium saucepan over medium heat. Add puree and bring to a boil, then turn heat to low. Add chocolate and stir to melt. Add broth or water and simmer for 15 to 20 minutes, stirring regularly, until flavors are well blended. Check every now and then on the thickness of the sauce, and add more water or broth if necessary.

Taste sauce and add more salt if needed. Stir in turkey meat, making sure to coat it completely. Cook 10 more minutes over low heat until turkey is hot and has absorbed some of the flavors. Serve with rice or leftover mashed potatoes.

Baked Maple Oatmeal

Food legend Marion Cunningham has a recipe for Oatmeal Pudding in her classic, The Breakfast Book. *I love it, but it takes an hour at least, which is a lot for breakfast. I turned to baked oatmeal to approximate her dish.*

SERVES **4**

1 3/4 cups rolled oats

1 1/2 cups milk

1/3 cup water

1 egg, lightly beaten

1/3 cup raisins or other dried fruit (optional)

1/2 tsp salt

2 Tbsp maple syrup

1 Tbsp butter (optional)

cinnamon-sugar mixture, for serving

Preheat oven to 375 degrees.

Butter a 9-inch pie dish (broiler-safe, e.g., not a Pyrex glass dish, if you plan to use in the broiler).

Mix all ingredients together in a bowl. Combine well. Pour into prepared dish and bake 30 minutes, until golden-brown on top. Remove pan from oven. If you want a really crunchy top, dot with the optional butter and place under the broiler for a minute or two.

Serve with milk or cream and cinnamon-sugar mixture.

Oats

My father claimed the world was divided into two groups of people: those who enjoy naps, and those who don't. I can't argue, but I think there may be another division: oatmeal lovers and oatmeal haters. We all know oatmeal is a terrifically nutritious food, full of fiber, protein, and even iron. Some people (including one of my kids) can't get past the texture, though, and avoid it like the plague. Climate-wise, oats are a good match for New England, but Maine is the only state in the region that grows them in any quantity. We invariably get oats in our winter farm share, and we get so many that we're always looking for something to do with them besides eat them for breakfast.

Raspberry Oat Squares

I like making fruit bars with fresh or frozen fruit instead of jam, because they taste fruitier to me. You just need to make sure the base is sturdy enough to support the topping. You can use other berries in this recipe. Vary the amount of sugar you use, depending on the sweetness of your berries, and adjust the amount of cornstarch you use to keep the topping from being too liquid. This recipe is a good way to use any berries you picked and froze over the summer.

MAKES **16** SQUARES

1/2 cup whole wheat flour

3/4 cups white flour

3/4 cups rolled oats, divided (not instant or quick)

2/3 cup sugar, divided

1/2 tsp salt

12 Tbsp butter, room temperature, divided, and cut into 12 1-tablespoon pieces

2 Tbsp brown sugar

1/2 tsp cinnamon

1/2 tsp vanilla

1 1/2 cups raspberries, fresh or frozen

2 tsp cornstarch if using fresh berries, 1 Tbsp if frozen

1 Tbsp lemon juice

Preheat oven to 375 degrees. Grease an 8 x 8-inch baking pan.

Base
Put both flours, 1/4 cup oats, 1/3 cup sugar, and salt in a bowl and mix gently to combine. With mixer on low, gradually add 10 table-spoons of butter to the flour mixture and mix until mixture is crumbly and no large butter pieces are visible. Scoop 2 cups of the mixture into the baking pan and pat firmly so that the bottom of pan is covered. Bake 12 to 14 minutes, then remove from oven. The crust should look dry but not brown.

Topping
Add the remaining 2 tablespoons butter, 1/2 cup of oats, brown sugar, cinnamon, and vanilla to remaining flour mixture. Mix until combined; it will look crumbly.

Place raspberries in a medium bowl and toss with remaining 1/3 cup sugar, cornstarch, and lemon juice. After bottom crust has baked, spread raspberry mixture on top.

Sprinkle topping over the raspberries. Return to oven and bake another 25 to 35 minutes, until nicely browned and crisp-looking on top. Cool on rack for 20 minutes before cutting into squares. Chilling them in the refrigerator will make it even easier to cut into clean-looking squares. Store uneaten squares, wrapped, in the refrigerator.

SAVORY OATMEAL

Here in the United States we normally sweeten oatmeal with dried fruit, brown sugar, or maple syrup. But there's no reason it has to be that way; oats are just another grain, and can be eaten like rice. In Scotland, a land famous for its oat consumption, one traditional way to serve oatmeal is simply with salt and butter, and perhaps a poached egg on top. You can also cook oats with onion and butter and serve as a side dish.

Sweetly Roasted Acorn Squash

A long time ago I worked at a farm stand in Massachusetts, and this is how the owner recommended cooking acorn squash. This method of "roasting" the squash actually involves steaming as well. You can use this method with other squash, too, although you need to adjust cooking times depending on their size and the thickness of their flesh. Feel free to vary the spice mix at the end.

SERVES **4** AS A SIDE DISH

2 acorn squash, halved and seeded

salt and pepper

4 Tbsp butter or olive oil

2 Tbsp brown sugar

1/2 tsp cinnamon

1/2 tsp cumin

1/4 tsp allspice

1/4 tsp ancho or other chili powder (optional)

Preheat oven to 400 degrees. Season insides of squash halves with salt and pepper. Pour enough water into a rimmed sheet pan to cover the bottom by 1/4 inch. Open oven and pull rack out; place pan on rack, and then place squash halves upside down on pan. (The reason for doing it in this order is to avoid lowering a sheet pan filled with water and heavy squash into a hot oven.) Close oven and bake for 35 minutes. Check the tenderness of the squash; it should be very soft. Continue baking for another 5 or 10 minutes, if needed, to finish cooking, and add additional water if the first batch has evaporated.

Meanwhile, melt the butter in a small saucepan. When melted, remove from heat and whisk in sugar, spices, and 1/2 tsp salt. Let sit off-heat until ready to use.

When squash is tender, remove from oven. Turn broiler to low. Whisk the spice mixture again to recombine. Flip the squash halves over, and brush the insides and top edges thoroughly with the butter/spice mixture. Place the halves under the broiler briefly until edges are browned. To eat, use a spoon to scoop out the flesh from the skin.

Winter Squash

Before farmer's markets, I was familiar with only a few kinds of winter squash: butternut, acorn, and Blue Hubbard (Blue Hubbard was the special giant squash we ate only at Thanksgiving). Also, I tended to cook squash in one of two ways: pureed in soup, or roasted with some melted butter and brown sugar for seasoning. It took the farmer's market to make me realize there are many varieties of winter squash, and that some of the lesser-known types are quite a bit tastier than the supermarket standards. (Personally, I've become partial to one called "Long Island Cheese.") I encourage you to branch out. Different squashes vary in the density of their flesh, their sweetness, and their consistency. Certain types are better for certain preparations; for instance, I wouldn't steam acorn squash as it is too stringy. Others, like butternut, are very adaptable.

Polenta with Squash and Sausage

A few years ago I heard Russ Parsons, the longtime food editor for the Los Angeles Times, *describe this easy way of cooking polenta, the Italian dish of cooked stone-ground cornmeal. Instead of stirring it over a hot stove for an incredibly long time, or buying one of those logs of precooked polenta, you just bake it with very little attention—one of my favorite cooking methods for any food. You can use a variety of vegetables here, but the sweetness of squash goes well with corn.*

SERVES 6 TO 8

4 1/2 cups water

salt

1 1/4 cups polenta (or substitute medium or coarsely ground cornmeal)

2 Tbsp butter

1 cup grated cheddar cheese (or use Parmesan cheese, or a mix)

pepper

8 cups winter squash, peeled and cut into 1-inch cubes

2 medium onions, cut into 8 wedges

2 Tbsp butter, melted

8 whole garlic cloves, peeled

2 tsp dried rosemary and/or sage

1/4 tsp nutmeg

1/4 tsp sugar

8 sausages (any kind)

1/2 cup minced parsley (optional)

Polenta

Preheat oven to 375 degrees. Stir water, 1 teaspoon salt, polenta, and butter together in a 3- or 4-quart ovenproof saucepan or deep casserole dish. Stir well so that no dry lumps of polenta remain. Bake uncovered for 1 hour. Stir very well, and bake another 10 minutes, until all liquid is absorbed and polenta is very soft. Stir in cheese and season with pepper. Let rest 5 minutes before serving.

Squash and sausages

Put squash and onions on a rimmed baking sheet. Pour butter over the vegetables, sprinkle with 1 teaspoon salt, and stir to coat. Spread vegetables in a single layer. Roast in the same 375-degree oven for 15 minutes.

Add garlic to baking sheet. Increase oven temperature to 425 degrees. (It's okay if the polenta is still in the oven, as long as it's during its last 20 minutes of cooking.) Season vegetables with rosemary and/or sage, nutmeg, sugar, and 1/2 teaspoon pepper. Give the vegetables a good stir. Nestle sausages among vegetables on tray and return to oven for 20 minutes. Remove pan and stir, in particular rotating the sausages so they brown on the other side. If pan looks very dry, pour a table-spoon of water in it, and scrape up any browned bits from the bottom. Return pan to oven and roast another 15 minutes. Check to make sure sausages are browned and vegetables tender; if not, return to oven for another 5 or 10 minutes.

When everything is done, remove tray and put sausages and vegetables together in a serving dish. Sprinkle parsley on top. Serve by placing a large scoop of polenta on each person's plate and topping each portion with a sausage and a share of roasted vegetables.

Stuffed Delicata Squash

I was never a huge fan of stuffed squash—until I learned that if you roast the squash empty first, the whole thing tastes much better. Delicata is great for stuffing because the squash cooks quickly, and you can eat the skin. This recipe is flexible. You can leave out or add more things as you wish; I like having kale in there, but it does get kind of chewy after being baked. Try more mushrooms, quinoa, or even a chopped-up apple instead.

SERVES **4** TO **6** AS A MAIN DISH

1 cup chopped pecans
(or substitute another nut)

1 lb mushrooms, cleaned and
sliced 1/4-inch thick

2 Tbsp olive oil, plus more
for brushing

salt and pepper

1/4 to 1/2 cup minced parsley
or other fresh herbs, if available

3 medium or 2 large delicata
squash, halved lengthwise and
seeded

1 cup quinoa

4 cups water

3 cups kale, stemmed and chopped

1/2 cup dried cranberries

1 cup crumbled feta cheese

2 tsp lemon juice

1/4 cup Parmesan cheese

Preheat oven to 425 degrees. Spread nuts on a small baking sheet and toast until fragrant, 4 or 5 minutes. Cool.

Toss mushrooms with olive oil, 1/4 teaspoon salt, and 1/4 teaspoon pepper. Spread on a baking sheet. Place in oven and roast for 15 minutes. Stir, then roast another 10 minutes, until mushrooms are browned and liquid has evaporated. Remove from oven. Toss mushrooms with chopped herbs in a large bowl and set aside.

At the same time, place squash halves skin side down on a foil-lined baking tray. Brush the inside of each with olive oil and sprinkle each with a pinch of salt and pepper. Roast them, in the same oven as the mushrooms, until squash is tender (but not collapsed) and lightly browned, about 20 minutes. Remove. Lower oven heat to 375 degrees.

Cook quinoa in 4 cups of salted boiling water for 5 minutes. Add chopped greens and continue simmering until greens are tender, about 10 more minutes. The quinoa will be done at this point, too. Drain well and add to mushrooms.

Add nuts, cranberries, feta cheese, and lemon juice to mushroom/quinoa mixture. Stir to combine well. Taste and season with salt and pepper, if needed. Fill each squash half with filling and top each with a sprinkle of grated Parmesan cheese. Return to oven (375 degrees) and bake 15 minutes, until brown on top.

Squash and Bean Soup

My son Harry "invented" this soup, although his version had only potatoes and no squash. Nonetheless, he would like proper credit. This soup goes well with a side of "cheesy toast" (toasted bread broiled with cheese on top), which I invented. At least that's what I told my kids.

SERVES **6**

1 cup dried beans
(any kind will do)

2 cups water

1 tsp salt, divided

bay leaf

2 Tbsp olive oil

1 Tbsp butter

1/2 medium onion, diced

2 carrots, diced or cut into
coins or half-moons

1 potato, peeled and cut into
3/4-inch dice

3 garlic cloves, pressed or smashed

1 tsp dried thyme

1 1/2 tsp cumin

1/2 tsp smoked paprika

1/2 tsp sugar

1/2 cup white wine or vermouth

3 cups water or vegetable broth

3 cups winter squash (peeled
and cut into 3/4-inch dice)

1/2 tsp white pepper

1 Tbsp cider vinegar, or more
to taste

Put beans in a small saucepan with 2 cups water, 1/2 teaspoon salt, and bay leaf. Bring to a boil and simmer, covered, until beans are tender, about 45 minutes for presoaked beans, 90 minutes for unsoaked (see the **Prepping Dried Beans** tip on page 63 for details). The exact time will depend on the size and freshness of the beans, so check them regularly. Remove from heat and remove bay leaf. Drain beans, reserving cooking liquid.

Place olive oil and butter in a large saucepan or Dutch oven over medium heat. When foaming subsides, add onion, carrot, and 1/2 teaspoon salt. Cook, stirring regularly, until onions start to brown, about 5 minutes. Add potato, garlic, thyme, cumin, paprika, and sugar. Stir to coat. When mixture is sizzling and fragrant, add wine and let it cook off for a few minutes, until the aroma of alcohol dissipates. Add broth or water and bring to a boil. Lower heat and simmer 5 minutes. Add beans and squash and simmer an additional 15 minutes, or until vegetables are fully tender. If at any point the soup seems too thick, add some of the leftover cooking water from the beans.

If desired, puree a cup or two of the soup and then add it back, to give it a thicker consistency. Add white pepper and vinegar. Adjust seasonings. Serve with a dollop of sour cream or yogurt.

ROASTING A WHOLE SQUASH

Sometimes bringing a squash home from the farmer's market can be intimidating. When I look at one of those giant turban squashes, I picture how I'll have to hack it open with a cleaver and then spend a ton of time peeling it. One way to avoid all that is to pierce the whole squash a few times with a sharp knife and then chuck the whole thing in the oven on a foil-lined sheet pan. You can roast the squash while doing other things—even cooking other things in the oven— and at the end, the soft, cooked squash will be relatively easy to dissect.

January

parsnips

rutabaga

cabbage

dried beans

January

IT'S THE HEART OF WINTER and one of our snowiest months. One can only imagine California's farmer's markets, tables heaped high with tangelos and oranges. At a New England farmer's market, the juiciest item you're likely to find is a carrot. It's a challenge to eat both fresh and local.

The good news is that more and more winter farmer's markets are sprouting up in the region as farmers invest in greenhouses to extend the growing season. Though cold air and low amounts of sunlight limit the range of even hothouse crops, fresh, hardy greens such as kale and lettuce are often available.

January is a good month to dip into that stored produce and use the items raw, while they still retain some snap. People don't often eat rutabaga raw, but it's actually sweet and crunchy. Cabbage, although not always sweet, does not have to be drenched in mayonnaise and buttermilk to enjoy it raw. It stays crisp when thrown into a salad or when tossed with vinegar and served as a slaw. A little crunch at the table provides a great contrast to all those tasty roasted vegetables you're dishing up.

Sweet-and-Sour Cabbage

Traditional Scandinavian sweet-and-sour red cabbage is cooked for hours on the stove; this makes it very soft and tasty, but also takes a long time—and it's almost always made with red cabbage. The following recipe is nontraditional, but it's fast(er), and you can use any color cabbage you want. Whole cloves are a traditional seasoning, but feel free to substitute ground cloves. Scandinavians don't pick out the whole cloves before serving, but you might want to.

SERVES 4 TO 6 AS A SIDE DISH

1 medium or large head cabbage, tough outer leaves removed, cored and chopped into 1/2-inch-thick slices

1 1/2 tsp salt, divided

2 tsp brown sugar

2 Tbsp Worcestershire sauce

3 Tbsp olive oil

1/2 cup apple cider or apple, orange, or cranberry juice

6 whole cloves or 1/2 tsp ground cloves

1 Tbsp honey

1/3 cup cider vinegar or rice wine vinegar

1 Tbsp lemon juice

1/2 teaspoon pepper

2 Tbsp butter

Preheat oven to 400 degrees.

Pile the sliced cabbage on two rimmed baking sheets. Mix 1 teaspoon salt, brown sugar, Worcestershire sauce, and olive oil in a small bowl. Pour half over each pile of cabbage. Toss the cabbage well to coat, then spread out across the baking sheets. Roast 15 minutes, remove from oven, and stir. Roast another 5 to 10 minutes, until somewhat browned.

Meanwhile, make the sauce. Put cider or juice in a small skillet with the cloves, and boil until reduced by half, about 5 to 10 minutes. Remove the whole cloves now if you want. Add honey, vinegar, lemon juice, 1/2 teaspoon salt, and pepper. Simmer until somewhat thick-ened, about 10 minutes. Stir in butter. Remove from heat and reserve until cabbage is done roasting.

To assemble the dish, scrape the hot cabbage into a large serving bowl. Pour sauce over, and toss until evenly coated. Adjust seasonings to taste.

Cabbage

Cabbage too often appears in a limp coleslaw piled next to fish and chips, which is a shame for such a versatile vegetable. Many people experiment with making sauerkraut, which transforms cabbage into a fermented concoction filled with beneficial bacteria. I like cabbage in almost all its applications, and I think most people can find at least one they enjoy.

Fårikål (Lamb in Cabbage)

This stew is the national dish of Norway. It is neither fancy nor pretty, and to enjoy it you need to tolerate whole peppercorns in your finished dish. Norwegians will mock you mercilessly if you complain about those peppercorns. If you can take all that, you will wind up with a hearty, rewarding meal. And if your farmer's market sells mutton, this is the place to use it in place of lamb. In any case, you'll need lamb still on the bone, and cut into chunks. Note to nitpickers: The onion is not traditional. But my Uncle Rølf said it was okay, so who are we to argue?

SERVES **6**

1 1/2 large heads cabbage, tough outer leaves removed, cored, and cut into 2-inch-thick slices

1 yellow onion, peeled and sliced 1/4-inch thick

4-lb lamb shoulder, shank, or neck (at least some pieces on the bone), cut into 2- to 3-inch chunks

1 Tbsp salt

5 tsp whole black peppercorns (or use 1 Tbsp cracked black pepper)

4 cups water

Preheat oven to 300 degrees.

Place a layer of cabbage slices on the bottom of a Dutch oven (or stovetop safe casserole dish). Top with a layer of onion, and then a layer of lamb meat. Sprinkle with salt and whole peppercorns. Cover with a layer of cabbage, sprinkle with more salt and peppercorns. Repeat layering process until all ingredients are used up, ending with a layer of cabbage. Add 4 cups of water. Bring to a boil on the stovetop, cover tightly, and place in oven.

Cook for several hours (at least 2 and as many as 4), until lamb is tender and falling off the bone. Check every hour or so to make sure the dish isn't getting too dry; if necessary, add water. Serve with boiled potatoes and lingonberry jam or cranberry relish. The sweetness and acidity of some fruit on the side is a must. Leftover fårikål will taste even better as the flavors develop overnight.

Vinegary Cabbage Slaw

Coleslaw, whether based in mayonnaise, buttermilk, or vinegar, tends to develop a puddle of liquid at the bottom of the bowl after a while. Pre-salting and draining the shredded cabbage helps avoid this, but takes a lot of time, if not much work. If you don't have time to pre-salt and drain, try this recipe. It's quicker, and results in a much smaller puddle, which is easily folded back into the slaw.

SERVES **4** AS A SIDE DISH

1/2 small or 1/4 large head cabbage, tough outer leaves and core removed, sliced thinly or shredded

1 or 2 carrots, shredded

1 small rutabaga, peeled and shredded (optional)

1 small onion, finely chopped

3/4 tsp salt

2 tsp extra virgin olive oil

2 Tbsp cider vinegar or rice wine vinegar

1/2 tsp honey or sugar

1/2 tsp dry mustard

1/4 tsp pepper

lemon juice, to taste

Combine cabbage, carrots, rutabaga, onion, and salt in a large serving bowl and mix well. In a small bowl, whisk together olive oil, vinegar, honey, mustard, and pepper. Drizzle over cabbage and toss well. This will not seem like enough dressing. Don't panic. Let bowl sit at room temperature for about 30 minutes. Then stir again, incorporating the liquid collected at the bottom of the bowl. Drizzle with lemon juice and adjust for salt and pepper.

SAUERKRAUT

Sandor Katz and others in his field have been bringing more attention to the importance and tastiness of fermented foods. Sauerkraut is one of these. It has been proven to contain helpful bacteria and lots of vitamin C, and it shows up in all sorts of traditional American and northern European meals. Although I'm fond of it, I've only made sauerkraut a few times, following Katz's easy instructions on his website (www.wildfermentation.com). It's a great way to use any extra cabbage you might have.

Pasta e Fagioli (Pasta and Beans)

Mixing pasta with beans in the same dish makes perfect sense, especially in winter. Beans provide protein and fiber; pasta provides a nice chewiness. Together they make a very comforting meal. This basic formula varies widely throughout Italy. Change yours as you see fit, using firmer or softer beans, different shapes of pasta, or different seasonings (sage is very good), and making it soupier or thicker.

JANUARY / 62

SERVES **4** TO **6**

3 cups vegetable broth

4 slices bacon, diced

4 cups cooked beans (from 1 1/2 cups dried; see **Prepping Dried Beans** tip on page 63)

salt and pepper

1 cup (about 6 oz) small uncooked pasta, like ditalini or mini farfalle, or even broken spaghetti strands

1 Tbsp plus 1 tsp extra virgin olive oil, divided

1 Tbsp butter

1 small onion, chopped small

1 rib celery, chopped small

1 carrot, chopped small

3 cloves garlic, pressed or minced

1/2 tsp dried crushed rosemary

1/2 tsp red pepper flakes

2 Tbsp tomato paste

grated Parmesan or pecorino cheese, for serving

Heat broth to boiling, then keep warm over low heat.

Heat bacon in a medium skillet over medium heat. Cook until bacon fat has mostly rendered and meat is browned, about 6 minutes. If there is more than 1 tablespoon of fat in the pan, pour off any excess. Add beans to skillet and stir to coat. Add 3/4 cup broth, scraping the bottom of the pan to incorporate any browned bits. Cook until liquid is mostly evaporated. Adjust for salt and pepper and remove from heat.

Meanwhile, cook pasta until very al dente. It should be significantly firmer or chewier than you would want it if you were eating it right away. Drain and toss with a teaspoon of olive oil to prevent sticking.

Dried Beans

The impetus for this book actually came from dried beans. I overheard our CSA organizer bemoan the arrival of 5 pounds of dried beans. "I still have beans from last year's box!" she sighed. I realized that if the person organizing the CSA had difficulty finding ways to cook the contents of her weekly box, then others might too, and there might be a niche for a cookbook like this one. Dried beans come in all kinds of colors and shapes. Different varieties do work better in different preparations. Some stay firmer when cooked, so are preferred for soups, while others fall apart, and are better for baked beans. In these recipes, you can experiment with what you have on hand. As you get to know the types better, you'll probably develop preferences for which kind to use, when.

Melt butter and remaining tablespoon olive oil in a large skillet over medium heat. Add onion, celery, and carrot and cook, stirring occasionally, until they become tender and begin to brown, about 8 minutes. Stir in garlic, rosemary, and pepper flakes. Cook 30 seconds. Add tomato paste and cook, stirring constantly, for 2 minutes. Add 3/4 cup broth and cook at a low boil, again until almost evaporated, scraping the bottom of the pan to incorporate any browned bits. Add the bean and bacon mixture and a cup of broth to the vegetables and simmer briskly.

When pasta is ready, add to the mixture along with the last bit of broth. Continue simmering until pasta is fully cooked. Add more liquid if you prefer the dish soupier. Adjust seasoning. Serve with grated Parmesan or pecorino cheese.

PREPPING DRIED BEANS

Opening a can of beans is, admittedly, a lot easier than using dried beans. But dried beans, aside from (potentially) being locally grown, have major advantages in taste, texture, and cost. While they do require advance planning, there isn't much work involved.

My favorite method is adapted from *Cook's Illustrated*. In the morning, put your beans in a medium bowl and add a teaspoon or two of salt. Add cool water to cover beans by at least 2 inches, and stir to dissolve the salt. In the evening, drain the beans and put in a saucepan. Cover with water by an inch, and bring to a boil. Reduce heat to a simmer, cover, and cook until beans are tender, 45 minutes to 75 minutes, depending on your beans, adding more water if you need to. Local dried beans will tend to cook more quickly, as they are more likely to be relatively fresh. Once they are cooked, beans freeze well, so you can always make extra and have them ready for your next recipe.

Beans with Bacon and Red Wine Sauce

This is a variation on baked beans, switching out bacon for the salt pork and red wine for the molasses. I'm very fond of baked beans, but sometimes you need a change.

SERVES **4** TO **6** AS A SIDE DISH

2 cups dried beans, presoaked and drained (about 3 1/2 cups cooked beans)

4 oz bacon, diced

1 to 2 Tbsp butter, if needed

1 small onion, diced

1 carrot, diced

salt

1 bay leaf

1/2 tsp ground coriander

3 cloves garlic, pressed or minced

1 cup red wine

6 pitted prunes, chopped

1 tsp balsamic vinegar

1/2 tsp pepper

Cook beans until tender (see **Prepping Dried Beans** tip on page 63). Drain, reserving a cup of the cooking water.

While beans cook, make the sauce. Put bacon in a medium skillet and bring to medium heat. Cook, stirring occasionally, until fat has rendered and bacon is crisp, about 5 minutes. If you have more than 2 tablespoons of bacon fat in the pan, pour some off; if you have less, add butter to bring the amount of fat to about 2 tablespoons. Turn heat to medium-low and add onion, carrot, 1/4 teaspoon salt, bay leaf, and coriander. Cook until vegetables are softened, stirring frequently, about 6 minutes.

Add garlic and stir into vegetables. Pour in red wine, scraping bottom to incorporate any browned bits. Bring to a boil, then lower heat to a simmer. Add prunes and simmer until sauce has cooked down quite a bit and prunes are very soft, about 8 minutes. Remove skillet from heat and discard bay leaf.

When beans are ready, return skillet to low heat. Add 1/2 cup of the cooked beans to skillet and mash them with a fork to give the dish some body. You can also stir in some of the reserved bean water to make it moister. Add remainder of the beans, vinegar, and pepper. Cook for a few minutes to combine flavors. Adjust salt and pepper. Serve beans with rice or other mild starch.

Parsnip Muffins

Americans love their carrot cakes and muffins, but in the rest of the world, carrots are not often used for dessert, and many people find the idea of carrot cake unappetizing. (One of my visiting Norwegian cousins thought the carrot cake listed on a restaurant's menu was a joke.) Americans probably feel the same way about baking with parsnips, but there's really no reason for the discrimination, as the two roots are so similar. You could increase the sugar a bit in this recipe and add frosting, and you'd have parsnip cupcakes. Why not?

MAKES **12** MUFFINS

1 cup all-purpose flour

1/2 cup whole wheat flour

1 tsp baking powder

1/2 tsp baking soda

1 tsp cinnamon

1/2 tsp nutmeg

1/2 tsp ground cloves

1/2 tsp salt

1/2 cup applesauce

1/3 cup vegetable oil

5 Tbsp butter, melted

1/4 cup milk

1 tsp vanilla

2 eggs

1/2 cup sugar

1/2 cup brown sugar

2 1/2 cups shredded, peeled parsnips (about 4 medium)

Preheat oven to 350 degrees.

Put both flours, baking powder, baking soda, spices, and salt in a medium bowl and whisk to combine.

Mix applesauce, vegetable oil, butter, milk, and vanilla in a large measuring cup. In a mixing bowl, beat eggs and sugars on medium speed with the paddle for about 2 minutes, until very well blended. Pour in liquid ingredients and mix well again, about 30 seconds. Add dry ingredients in three additions, mixing gently after each. Fold in parsnips.

Line a muffin tin with paper liners. Scoop in batter. Bake 24 minutes and check for doneness (a toothpick poked into the middle should come out clean). Let baked muffins rest for 5 minutes in the tin, on a baking rack. Remove muffins from tin and cool, or eat right away.

Parsnips

I have heard it said that parsnips were once America's carrots. They were the preferred long, pointy root vegetable because they stored much better than carrots in the days before refrigerators. They definitely have a more interesting, spicier flavor than carrots. Although parsnips originated in the Mediterranean, they do very well in cold climates. This is great news for New Englanders, because parsnips are excellent in cold-weather comfort foods like stews and roasts. Be careful with larger parsnips, as their interior can get woody and unpleasant to chew. My rule of thumb is to trim out the core of any parsnip with a diameter of more than an inch. I cut the parsnip into quarters, lengthwise, and run a knife down the core to remove it. You don't have to get every last bit of the core, just the bulk of it.

Pot Roast with Horseradish

This recipe takes a long time. Long, slow cooking is a good way to get a nice supper out of a less-expensive cut of beef. And less-expensive cuts of meat have long been favored by frugal New Englanders. You can raise the oven temperature a bit to make the cooking go faster, but I'm not sure what the hurry is. Is the horseradish some New England tradition? I don't know, but it tastes good, and horseradish does grow here, so let's say yes.

SERVES **6**

1 3- to 4-lb beef chuck roast

salt and pepper

2 Tbsp olive oil

1 medium or large onion, chopped

6 parsnips or carrots (or a mix), peeled, half of them chopped, half cut into 2-inch chunks

1 bulb celeriac, if you have it, peeled and chopped

1 6-oz jar prepared horseradish (or home-preserved horseradish, if you know someone who does that)

6 cloves garlic, smashed

2 Tbsp tomato paste

2 to 4 cups water or low-sodium broth (beef or vegetable)

2 turnips, peeled and cut into 2-inch chunks

1 rutabaga, peeled and cut into 2-inch chunks

1 Tbsp cider vinegar

Remove the roast from the refrigerator and pat dry with paper towels. The drier it is, the better it will brown. Season liberally with salt and pepper.

Preheat oven to 300 degrees.

Heat olive oil in a sturdy Dutch oven over medium heat. Put the roast in the pot and brown it, without moving, for 4 to 5 minutes. Then, using tongs, turn the roast on its next side and brown that side. Continue until all sides are browned. You may need to lower the heat a little if the bottom of the pot starts to get too dark.

Remove the roast to a plate. Put the onion, chopped parsnips/carrots, and celeriac in the Dutch oven. If the bottom of the pot is getting very dark, add a couple of tablespoons of water and scrape the browned bits off the bottom. Cook the vegetables, stirring every so often, until onions are somewhat tender and beginning to brown. Use part of this cooking time to smear the horseradish over the top and sides of the resting beef. You don't have to use all the horseradish if you're feeling unsure, but it loses almost all its sharpness during the cooking process.

Add garlic and tomato paste to pot and cook, stirring, for 2 minutes. Add 2 cups of water to the pot and scrape the bottom to incorporate any browned bits. Return the roast to the pot along with any accumulated juices. Bring to a simmer. If you have it, place a piece of parchment paper across the top of the pot, and then cover tightly with lid. If not, just use the lid. Put covered pot in oven.

After 30 minutes, check the liquid to make sure it is simmering. If it's boiling, lower heat to 275 degrees; if it's just sitting there, increase temperature to 310 or 320 degrees. Cook for another hour. Baste the top of the roast with some of the liquid in the pot. There should still be at least 2 cups of liquid in the pot, but if the level of liquid is looking low, add a cup of water.

Cook another hour. Baste the top of the roast again. Add the remaining parsnips/carrots, turnips, and rutabaga. Check the liquid level again, keeping in mind that the vegetables will release liquid while they cook. Cook another hour, then check to see if the meat and vegetables are tender enough; cook longer if necessary. When completely cooked, remove from oven and stir in vinegar. Season to taste. To use even more root vegetables, serve with mashed potatoes.

HOW TO HAVE A SHRIMP PARTY

We may not harvest fresh citrus in January, but New England does have something special this time of year—namely, Maine shrimp, whose season usually runs from January to March. These sweet, delicate crustaceans are sadly underrated. One excellent way to serve them is to mimic the Scandinavians, and host a *rekefest*, or shrimp party. (Yes, Norwegians have a special word for "shrimp party.")

The necessary ingredients are simple: a pile of cooked Maine shrimp in the shell (if you're lucky, you can get your fishmonger to cook the shrimp for you—or if you're even luckier, find a fisherman to cook them on board the boat, in seawater); several crusty baguettes; mayonnaise; lemon wedges; and a lot of chilled white wine. Figure on at least a half-pound of shrimp per person, and probably more.

Here's how it goes: Put several big bowls of shrimp on the table. Guests take a heap of shrimp onto their plates. They all prepare a slice of baguette with a good smear of mayonnaise. Then they peel their shrimp. I was taught to hold the shrimp in my left hand and pinch the head off with my right, twisting a little. Then pull all the legs off to one side and continue around, peeling the back shell off. Finally, pull the little tail off. (There are videos of this procedure on YouTube if you need assistance.) Now you have one clean shrimp, which you place on your baguette, or surreptitiously eat because you are hungry.

When you have a good pile of shrimp on your bread, spritz some lemon over it, and eat the open-faced sandwich with gusto. You will be hungry after having peeled all that shrimp! It takes a lot of tiny Maine shrimp to make a sandwich. A *rekefest* is messy, decidedly unkosher, and well-known for promoting a lot of wine consumption and good conversation. You should host at least one *rekefest* each year. To add a fancy touch to the party, make your own mayonnaise, offer sprigs of dill, and serve salad or some other vegetable to make it "healthier."

Chicken Cutlets with Fried Parsnips and Apples

Fried apples? Yes. You can leave them out if you want, but if you have storage apples on hand, they are nice with parsnips. You can make your own chicken cutlets from boneless, skinless chicken breasts: First, cut off the extra flap of meat (the tenderloin), then cut the remaining breast in half horizontally. Now you have three cutlets, two big ones and one little one. You don't need to pound them flat unless you want to.

SERVES **6**

3 boneless, skinless chicken breasts, cut into cutlets

salt and pepper

2 eggs

2 Tbsp mustard, Dijon or whole-grain, divided

2 cups panko (Japanese bread crumbs)

3 Tbsp olive oil

3/4 tsp chili powder, divided

6 medium to large parsnips, peeled

3 Tbsp butter

1/2 tsp dried thyme

2 Tbsp sherry

1/4 cup apple cider

2 or 3 apples

2 Tbsp maple syrup

2 tsp lemon juice

Preheat oven to 400 degrees. Place a wire rack over a rimmed baking sheet and spray rack lightly with cooking spray.

Remove cutlets from refrigerator, pat dry with paper towels, and season with salt and pepper.

In one shallow dish, beat the eggs well with 1 tablespoon mustard and 1/4 teaspoon salt. In a second shallow dish, mix the panko, olive oil, 1/4 teaspoon chili powder, 1/4 teaspoon salt, and 1/4 teaspoon pepper together. Dip each cutlet first into beaten egg, allowing excess to drip off, then into crumbs. Use your hands to press the coating all over the chicken. Place cutlet on wire rack. Repeat with all pieces. Bake the two little cutlets (if using) for 15 to 20 minutes; bake the larger ones for 25 to 30 minutes. They should be browned and crisp, and have an interior temperature of 160 degrees.

While the chicken bakes, prepare the parsnips and apples. Cut the parsnips so that all pieces are approximately the same thickness. (One way is to cut the parsnips into thirds, horizontally. Leave the tip pieces alone. Halve the center pieces lengthwise, and trim away the core. Cut the stouter top pieces into quarters lengthwise and trim away the core. If you have a parsnip with a funky shape, you may have to use a different method.) Heat butter in large skillet over medium heat. When foaming subsides, add parsnips, thyme, and remaining 1/2 teaspoon chili powder and cook without stirring for 3 minutes. Stir once, then cook undisturbed another 2 minutes. Add sherry and cider and cook, stirring a few times, for 3 minutes.

While the parsnips are cooking, prepare the apples by peeling them, coring them, and cutting each into eight wedges. After parsnips have cooked in the sherry and cider for 3 minutes, add the apples and 1/2 teaspoon salt to the pan, stirring every so often. After 3 minutes, add the maple syrup, lemon juice, and remaining tablespoon mustard. Stir to incorporate ingredients and cook a few more minutes, as apples get tender and sauce thickens. Remove from heat and season with salt and pepper. Serve parsnips and apples as a side to the chicken. It's especially nice to take a bite of chicken with a bite of parsnip or apple at the same time.

Rutabaga with Bean Dip

Raw rutabaga has an unappreciated sweetness. If you can prepare this and not let people see the intact rutabaga ahead of time, they will think they are eating some kind of delicious exotic vegetable. By the way, the dip includes ketchup, meaning my mother would officially disassociate herself from it. But her grandkids love it.

SERVES **4** AS AN APPETIZER, with dip left over

1 1/2 cups cooked red beans (or other beans), divided

1/4 cup sour cream

2 Tbsp mayonnaise

2 Tbsp pickle relish or chopped-up pickle (sweet or dill, as you prefer)

1 Tbsp ketchup

1 tsp red wine vinegar

a few drops Worcestershire sauce

1 tsp prepared horseradish

1 Tbsp minced onion or shallot

1 small garlic clove, minced

1 large rutabaga, raw, peeled and cut into 1/4-inch-thick matchsticks

Microwave (or heat on the stove) 1 cup of the beans until hot. Puree these beans in a food processor. Add all remaining ingredients except the rutabaga and the remaining whole beans, and process until smooth. Transfer to a dish and fold in the remaining whole beans. Use the rutabaga sticks and other vegetables for dipping.

Rutabaga

My mother is crazy about rutabaga, although it bewilders most people; it's weird-looking, and it goes by goofy names, including "swede" and "neep." Scandinavians and other northern Europeans are very fond of rutabaga; somehow it hasn't really caught on with Americans. It's a nutritious vegetable, though, and it grows well in New England, so it's really worth giving it a try. If you don't like the turnip-y taste straight, you can always mash it with potatoes. But I have found many people like rutabaga when cooked properly.

Rutabaga over Couscous

Rutabaga is terrific roasted; just make sure you cook it all the way through. And Israeli couscous (the really big couscous) is fun to eat. You can swap in other roots if you like; they all taste good in this application. You can use regular couscous if it's easier to find; just reduce the cooking time and use a one-to-one ratio of couscous to water.

SERVES 6 AS A SIDE DISH (if using chickpeas, can serve 4 as main course)

1 to 2 rutabagas, peeled and cut into 1-inch chunks (about 6 cups' worth)

5 Tbsp extra virgin olive oil, divided

1 1/2 tsp cumin, divided

2 Tbsp lemon juice

1/2 tsp sugar

1 1/2 tsp salt, divided

3 cloves garlic, pressed or minced

1 cup Israeli couscous

1 3/4 cups water

4 tsp honey

1 tsp oregano

1 Tbsp red wine vinegar

1/2 tsp smoked paprika

1 cup cooked chickpeas or other small bean

1/2 red onion, sliced thinly

finely minced fresh herbs, if available

pepper

Preheat oven to 375 degrees.

Put rutabaga on a rimmed baking sheet. In a small bowl, whisk together 2 tablespoons olive oil, 1 teaspoon cumin, lemon juice, sugar, and 1 teaspoon salt. Pour this dressing over the rutabaga and stir to coat. Roast in oven for 20 minutes. Remove and stir, then place back in oven for another 20 minutes or so, until vegetables are tender.

Meanwhile, make the couscous. Heat 2 tablespoons olive oil and garlic in a medium saucepan over medium heat, stirring regularly. When garlic is sizzling, add couscous and 1/2 teaspoon salt and stir to coat. Cook, stirring, for another 2 to 3 minutes, until couscous starts to smell a bit toasty. Add water and bring to a boil; turn heat to low, cover, and cook undisturbed for 15 minutes. Remove from heat and let sit, covered, another 5 minutes. Remove cover and fluff vigorously with a fork to allow steam to escape. Turn into large serving bowl, and drizzle with remaining tablespoon olive oil. Stir to incorporate.

To make the final dressing, whisk together honey, oregano, vinegar, remaining 1/2 teaspoon cumin, and smoked paprika.

Add the rutabaga, chickpeas, red onion, and herbs to couscous. Season with a grinding of pepper and then pour in final dressing. Fold a few more times to combine.

honey

turnips

cornmeal

February

potatoes

February

BY NOW, YOU MAY FIND that heavy winter stews aren't comforting anymore; instead, you're craving a supper of *insalata caprese* and fettuccine with fresh pesto. In February in New England, you may have to indulge with ingredients from warmer climates. But there are ways to make winter meals feel lighter without relying on trucked-in produce.

Soups, for instance, can be both soothing and light. If you skip the cream and pureeing, you can make a pot filled with vegetables and dumplings and achieve the epitome of comfort food without heaviness. Happily, winter's root vegetables give excellent flavor to broths. Put some bread and cheese on the table, and you have a satisfying winter meal without roasting or stewing.

Another way to brighten the table is to serve a vinegary side dish. Pickling and canning should ideally be done in the summer, when cucumbers or green beans are fresh. But you can always make a quick pickle in February, with turnips or rutabagas.

If you have signed up for a winter CSA, you may find some non-vegetable items at this point. We are always happy to peek in our box and see a jar of honey or a bag of cornmeal. Just browsing at a farmer's market may inspire you to pick up some new items—cheeses, preserves, or dried herbs, for instance. After pounds of potatoes, these things are downright festive. I guess it doesn't take much to get a cook excited during February in New England.

Cornmeal Blueberry Squares

If you have some frozen blueberries left over from summer picking, or if your farm share happens to provide you with some, these bars offer a nice blast of summer. The flavor of the corn and the berries might transport you right back to July.

MAKES **16** SMALL SQUARES

11 Tbsp butter

1/2 tsp vanilla

1/2 tsp lemon zest

1 cup plus 2 Tbsp flour

2/3 cup cornmeal

1 scant tsp baking powder

1/2 tsp salt

1/4 tsp ginger

1 cup sugar, divided

1 1/2 cups blueberries, fresh or frozen

4 tsp cornstarch

2 tsp lemon juice

Preheat oven to 350 degrees. Grease an 8 x 8-inch pan.

Melt the butter in a saucepan over low heat. Remove from heat and stir in vanilla and lemon zest.

Place the flour, cornmeal, baking powder, salt, ginger, and 3/4 cup of the sugar in a large bowl. Whisk briefly to combine, then pour in the melted butter mixture. Mix, leaving no dry spots of flour. Press about two-thirds of the mixture into the prepared pan. Bake for 20 minutes, until golden brown.

Meanwhile, prepare the blueberries. In a medium bowl, toss the blueberries, remaining 1/4 cup sugar, and cornstarch. Mix in lemon juice.

When bottom crust has baked, remove from the oven. Raise oven temperature to 375 degrees. Pour the berries over the bottom layer, then crumble the remaining cornmeal dough on top. Bake 30 minutes, until top is nicely browned. Cool in the pan, then cut into squares.

Cornmeal

Corn was the primary grain of the Americas for thousands of years. Botanically, it is pretty nifty, as it's a more efficient photosynthesizer than many other plants. There are many ways to use corn, from eating it on the cob to turning it into moonshine. Stone-ground cornmeal is usually a whole grain. It lacks gluten, so it won't create much structure if used alone (as you can see when eating grits or polenta, which are exclusively corn). But when combined with wheat flour, it has lots of uses.

Cornbread-Topped Bean Chili

You can top any favorite chili recipe with cornbread. The recipe below includes lots of beans plus some winter squash. I like to bake the cornbread in the pot with the chili, to save a dish during cleanup. You could also put the chili in a baking dish before topping with cornbread. Just remember that the surface area will determine how thick the cornbread is. The amount of batter below gives my large Dutch oven a 1-inch layer of cornbread.

SERVES **6** TO **8**

For the chili

2 1/2 cups dried beans, presoaked and drained (see **Prepping Dried Beans** tip on page 63), or 6 cups cooked beans

1 1/2 tsp salt, divided

2 bay leaves

8 garlic cloves, peeled, divided

2 medium to large onions, one quartered, one chopped

3 Tbsp corn oil

2 Tbsp tomato paste

2 Tbsp chili powder

1 tsp ancho chile powder

1 tsp cumin

1 tsp coriander

1/2 tsp cinnamon

1 Tbsp brown sugar

1/2 butternut or other firm squash or pumpkin, peeled and cut into 1 1/2-inch cubes (about 4 cups' worth)

Chili

If using dried beans, put them in a pot and cover with water by 2 inches. Add 1/2 teaspoon salt, bay leaves, four garlic cloves, and the quartered onion. Bring to a boil, reduce heat to a simmer, and cover. Check every now and then to see if beans need more liquid. Begin tasting for doneness after 45 minutes. The beans need to be fully cooked and tender, which could take up to 90 minutes. Remove bay leaves and onion and discard. When they are fully cooked, drain the beans, saving cooking liquid, and add them to the chili pot.

Heat oil in a large ovenproof pot over medium-high heat. Add chopped onion and cook, stirring, until beginning to brown, about 5 minutes. Lower heat to medium and add tomato paste and cook, stirring into onions, for 1 minute. Smash remaining four cloves of garlic and add to pot, along with spices, brown sugar, 1 teaspoon salt, squash, and 2 tablespoons water. Stir to coat and scrape brown bits off the bottom of the pot. Cook another minute or two, stirring constantly, until sizzling and fragrant and water has mostly evaporated.

A HANDFUL OF CORNMEAL

Cornmeal often gets stuck in the back of the cupboard, remaining there until someone decides to make cornbread at Thanksgiving, or notices that the box has become a home for meal moths. But cornmeal is healthful and makes a great addition to baked goods and other dishes. It contains no gluten, so it doesn't work as a perfect substitute for flour in baked goods. But you can swap 1/4 or 1/2 cup of flour for cornmeal in breads, muffins, and even cookies, to get a change of flavor, a bit of crunch, and to use some of that 5-pound bag that came with your winter CSA. Cornmeal is an excellent coating for baked or fried seafood and chicken. Cornmeal pancakes are delicious. Or whip up hush puppies, which use a lot of cornmeal. After a batch, you won't need to eat anything else for a week.

2 Tbsp water

1 15-ounce can diced tomatoes

1/3 cup ketchup

1 cup brown beer plus 1/2 cup
low-sodium chicken broth (or use
all broth)

1 small canned chipotle pepper
in adobo, plus 1 tsp adobo sauce

For the cornbread
1/2 cup all-purpose flour

1 cup cornmeal

1/2 tsp baking soda

3/4 tsp salt

6 Tbsp buttermilk (substitute
plain yogurt if you don't have
buttermilk)

1/2 cup very hot water

2 Tbsp butter, melted

1 tsp sugar

3/4 cup grated Monterey Jack or
cheddar cheese

sour cream and avocado
for serving

Add tomatoes plus their liquid, ketchup, beer and broth, chipotle pepper, and adobo sauce. Stir, scraping bottom again, and bring to a boil. Lower heat to a simmer and cook, uncovered, until squash is tender, about 20 minutes. If chili ever seems too dry, add some of the set-aside cooking liquid from the beans. (The chili will thicken during the baking process, so it's good to have a little more liquid than you would in a normal stovetop chili.) Remove from heat. Adjust seasonings as needed.

Cornbread
Preheat oven to 425 degrees. In a medium bowl, mix flour, cornmeal, baking soda, and 3/4 teaspoon salt. In a measuring cup, whisk together buttermilk, water, butter, and sugar. Immediately whisk liquid ingredients into dry ones, making sure no lumps remain. Dollop batter over the chili and sprinkle cheese on top. Bake uncovered 15 minutes or so, until cornbread is cooked through and browned on top.

Chili will be bubbling fiercely; let sit 5 minutes before serving. Serve with sour cream and/or chopped avocado.

Carrot Loaf Cake with Honey Glaze

This is nothing like traditional American carrot cake. The carrots are pureed to make this more like a pound cake.

MAKES **1** LOAF

2 medium carrots, peeled and chopped

1/4 cup plus 2 Tbsp milk

1 tsp vanilla

1/4 cup plus 2 Tbsp honey, divided

1 1/2 cups flour

2 tsp cornstarch or potato starch

1/2 tsp salt

1/2 tsp baking soda

1/2 tsp ginger

9 Tbsp butter, divided, at room temperature

1/2 cup sugar

2/3 cup brown sugar

2 eggs

1 egg yolk

3/4 cup raisins

1/2 cup confectioners' sugar

lemon juice (optional)

Preheat oven to 350 degrees. Butter and flour an 8- or 9-inch loaf pan.

Combine the carrots, milk, vanilla, and 1/4 cup of the honey in a food processor and puree until very smooth. In a medium bowl, whisk together flour, cornstarch, salt, baking soda, and ginger.

In a mixing bowl on medium-low speed, cream 8 tablespoons of the butter and both sugars for several minutes, until very light and fluffy. Scrape down bowl. Increase speed to medium, and add eggs and yolk one at a time, making sure to fully incorporate each. The mixture may look curdled; don't worry. Scrape down bowl.

On low speed, add one-third of the flour mixture, and mix enough so that only a few streaks of flour remain visible. Add half the carrot mixture, and mix until mostly combined. Repeat. Add the last third of the flour mixture, mix for 15 seconds, then stop mixer and scrape down bowl. Turn mixer to medium-high and beat for 10 to 20 seconds, until batter looks very smooth. Fold in raisins.

Honey

The variation in farmer's market honey comes from whichever flower the bees were most likely frequenting while collecting their nectar. In Maine (where the honey-bee is the state insect), we often see buckwheat, blueberry, and raspberry honeys, which differ in their color and aroma. In most cooked dishes, you won't spot the difference, but you will when you make a dish with a lot of honey, or when you eat it uncooked. In these recipes, you can use any variety of raw or processed honey. If you cook with honey often enough, you'll start to have some favorites.

Pour into prepared pan and bake 10 minutes. Lower heat to 325 degrees and bake 40 more minutes. If the cake still looks very wet, lower heat to 300 degrees and bake another 10 or 15 minutes, until a toothpick inserted in the loaf comes out clean. Cool on rack 20 minutes, then gently flip cake out of pan.

While cake is baking, make the glaze. Heat the remaining tablespoon butter and the remaining 2 tablespoons honey until butter has melted and honey has thinned. Mix to make sure they are well combined, then whisk in confectioners' sugar. When combined, remove from heat. If you want, add a squeeze of lemon juice and a dash of vanilla to the glaze.

After cake has come out of the pan, paint the top with the glaze. You can do two coats, letting the first one dry for a few minutes before applying the second. Or simply drizzle the glaze over the cake, letting it spill down the sides.

SUBSTITUTING HONEY FOR SUGAR

Whether honey is healthier than sugar is a matter for debate, but honey is the best sweetening option if you want something produced locally. It is not an equal substitute for sugar, however, particularly when baking. If the sugar in a recipe for a baked item is used for aerating, as when butter and sugar are creamed, honey is not going to be a good substitute. In other cases, it can work well, as long you as you reduce the liquid in the recipe by about 20 percent. Because baked goods tend to be moister when made with honey, it's not ideal for crispy cookies. And because honey browns more quickly than sugar, you may need to reduce your baking temperature by about 25 degrees, depending on how much honey you are using.

Honey Walnut Bars

Because they contain honey, my father liked to think of these bars as a health food, and he ate them before, during, or after his frequent handball games. He was a good handball player, and I don't think it's a coincidence. On the other hand, my brother would almost certainly prefer honey peanut bars, so feel free to make the substitution if you, too, have a peanut fanatic in your family. This recipe contains neither spices nor extracts, to highlight the subtle flavor of the honey.

MAKES **12** BARS

15 Tbsp butter, divided

1/2 tsp salt

2 Tbsp sugar

2/3 cup brown sugar, divided

1 1/2 cups all-purpose flour

1/2 cup whole wheat flour

1 tsp baking powder

2 1/2 cups walnuts (or other nuts), roughly chopped

2 Tbsp heavy cream

3/4 cup honey

Preheat oven to 350 degrees. Grease a 9 x 13-inch pan. If you have parchment paper, use it to line the pan as well. These bars get sticky.

In a medium saucepan over low heat, melt 13 tablespoons of the butter with the salt. Remove from heat and mix in white sugar and 1/3 cup brown sugar. Mix well. The butter may still seem separated from the sugar; that's okay. Gently mix in flours and baking powder, until thoroughly combined. Pat the mixture into the prepared pan and bake for 16 minutes, until edges are lightly browned.

Place walnuts on a rimmed sheet pan and toast them briefly in the same oven for 5 minutes. Let cool.

While crust is baking, prepare the topping. In a small saucepan, over medium heat, melt the remaining 2 tablespoons butter. Stir in the remaining 1/3 cup brown sugar, cream, and honey. Simmer 3 minutes, stirring occasionally. Stir in walnuts.

Pour topping over warm crust and spread evenly. Bake at 350 degrees for 10 minutes. Topping should be really bubbly. You may need to rotate your pan to get it bubbling evenly. Cool on a rack before cutting into bars with a sharp paring knife.

Potato Tart

This may sound like the heaviest tart you've ever heard of. But it really isn't. It was one of the most popular items I used to sell at my little table at the farmer's market. In this recipe, less starchy potatoes like redskins or fingerlings work best, since they don't completely fall apart. When buying puff pastry, try to buy a brand that uses only butter, not shortening. Or make your own, if you like rolling out dough.

MAKES 1 TART, SERVES 4
AS A SMALL MAIN COURSE

1/2 pkg frozen puff pastry
(one 9 1/2 x 10-inch sheet)

6 cups salted water

3 to 4 medium potatoes, peeled and sliced 1/4-inch thick (about 3 cups sliced potatoes)

3/4 cup sour cream

2 tsp cornstarch

1/2 tsp dried thyme

1/4 tsp salt

1/2 tsp black pepper

2 cloves garlic, sliced thinly

salt and pepper to taste

1 to 2 Tbsp extra virgin olive oil

Take out the puff pastry and let it thaw on the counter while you prepare the filling.

Place an empty baking sheet or a pizza stone in the oven, and preheat the oven to 425 degrees.

Bring water to boil in a medium saucepan. Add potatoes, reduce heat to a gentle boil, and cook for 7 to 10 minutes, until barely tender. Drain as carefully as possible to keep the slices intact.

Mix the sour cream with the cornstarch, thyme, salt, and pepper. Unfold pastry sheet onto a floured counter. Roll slightly to lengthen pastry to 12 inches long. Place pastry on an ungreased sheet pan. Prick all over with a fork. Spread sour cream mixture over the pastry sheet, leaving 1/2-inch margin on all sides. Scatter the garlic slices over the sour cream. Arrange the potato slices on top, as neatly as you like. Sprinkle with salt and pepper and drizzle olive oil over everything.

Place in oven, on top of preheated baking sheet. (The preheated sheet helps to brown the crust and keep it crisp.) Bake for 25 to 35 minutes, rotating once, until crust is dark golden brown and potatoes have started browning a little.

Potatoes

Mainers harvest more than 1.5 billion pounds of potatoes each year. Although maligned of late, potatoes are healthful, containing high amounts of vitamin C and potassium. Norwegians love them, and my mother tried to serve us boiled potatoes daily. (As a child in postwar Norway, she would bring boiled-potato sandwiches to school for lunch, spread with a thick layer of bacon fat. You won't find that recipe here.) In these recipes, either waxy or starchy potatoes are indicated, depending on whether the potatoes should stay intact or get crumbly. Starchy potatoes, which crumble, are often labeled "baking" potatoes, and include russets and Idahoes; waxy potatoes, which hold their shape, are sometimes called "boiling" potatoes, and include redskins, fingerlings, and new potatoes. In the middle are some of the most popular varieties, like Yukon Gold and the various colored potatoes (purple, yellow, pink, white), which can be used in any recipe.

Karl's Latkes (Potato Pancakes)

If you live in southern Maine, it's a good idea to befriend Karl Schatz and Margaret Hathaway. You'll get a lot of good food and conversation out of the relationship. On Ten Apple Farm, their homestead in Gray, just north of Portland, they produce all kinds of great things, including most of the vegetables mentioned in this cookbook, plus goat cheese and delightful children. Karl makes excellent latkes, and he's kindly allowed me to include his recipe. Karl says, "The recipe works with any potato variety, but best with one that's firm and slightly waxy—not mealy, like a baking potato. And don't undercook them; they're best when they're well done."

MAKES 20 TO 24 3-INCH LATKES, enough for 4 *chazzers* (Yiddish for "glutton") or 6 to 8 polite people

2 lbs potatoes (6 to 10 waxy potatoes, depending on their size), scrubbed and peeled if the skin is thick

2 medium onions

salt

2 eggs, beaten lightly

1/4 cup matzo meal (or bread crumbs)

pepper

canola oil or *schmaltz* (rendered chicken fat), or combination of the two

applesauce or sour cream, for serving

Grate the potatoes and onions either by hand or using the grating disk of a food processor. If you cut the vegetables to get them into the food processor tube, make the pieces as large as you can, to get the longest possible grated strands. Put the grated vegetables in a large mixing bowl and sprinkle with 1 teaspoon salt, mixing well to distribute the salt. Don't wash the food processor bowl yet.

Transfer the mixture to a colander and let it drain for 5 to 10 minutes, pressing occasionally to release liquid. Put about one-third of the drained potatoes and onions back into the bowl of the food processor and puree until smooth. Put the puree and the grated potatoes and onions back into the large mixing bowl. Add the eggs and matzo meal and mix well. Season with salt and pepper.

Preheat oven to 225 degrees. Heat 1/4 inch of canola oil or *schmaltz*, or a combination of the two oils, over medium-high heat until hot. Using a large wooden spoon, drop the potato mixture by spoonfuls into the hot oil, smoothing the top a little to flatten each latke. Fry, and flip, until well done on both sides.

Drain latkes on a brown paper bag on cooking sheet and place in a warm oven while cooking remaining latkes.

A note about serving: *Some people like their latkes with applesauce, some with sour cream. It's a choice you're going to have to make. Don't eat them with both at the same time.*

ROASTED POTATOES

Roasted potatoes are a delicious and easy side dish. Recipes differ on how large to cut the potatoes and how hot to keep the oven. I like to cut my roasted potatoes in 2-inch chunks, because while I love a crispy exterior, I also like some contrast with the interior. My husband Mark likes them very crispy, so he cuts the potatoes much smaller. In any case, if you want them browned, there are a couple of things you have to do. First, you need to use some fat to coat them. Olive oil is great. Second, don't crowd them in the pan. They should have enough room to spread out without overlapping. Use a hot oven. Some cooks go up as high as 475 degrees; I like 425, and 350 is the minimum. Finally, don't stir them more than once or twice during cooking. Cooking time will depend a lot on the type and size of the potatoes. Somewhere between 30 and 45 minutes usually works.

Jansson's Temptation

Who was Jansson, and what tempted him? He was likely a Scandinavian with a dish of creamy potatoes in front of him. Anchovies may scare some people off, but they melt away in the dish, and just leave behind an extra deliciousness. Some of you may be scared by the cream, as well, but once in a while you have to eat like a Norwegian. Waxier potatoes like new potatoes do better in this recipe. If you only have starchy ones, cut them a little bigger so they don't fall apart.

SERVES **6** TO **8** AS A SIDE DISH

3 Tbsp butter or (don't tell Mormor) olive oil, divided, plus butter for the pan

2 medium yellow onions, finely sliced

2 1/2 lbs (5 to 8, depending on size) medium to large potatoes, peeled and cut into 1/2-inch strips

10 to 15 anchovy fillets (see note below), rinsed well and patted dry

1 cup half-and-half, plus more if needed

1/2 cup bread crumbs

Preheat oven to 400 degrees. Butter a 9 x 11-inch shallow casserole dish or something similar.

Heat 2 tablespoons butter or oil in a skillet over medium heat and sauté onions with a pinch of salt until softened but not browned, about 6 minutes.

Layer one-third of the potato strips on the bottom of the casserole dish. Cover with half the onions, and scatter half the anchovies on top. Repeat, ending with the remaining third of the potato strips. Pour the half-and-half over the casserole, making sure to dampen the top layer of potatoes. There should be enough liquid to reach the top layer of potatoes, but not to cover them. Add more half-and-half if necessary.

Bake, uncovered, for 30 minutes. Remove from oven. Check liquid level; if it appears dry, add 1/4 cup more half-and-half. Use a spatula to push down the top layer of potatoes so they are moistened again. Sprinkle bread crumbs on top and dot with final tablespoon butter (or drizzle with olive oil). Bake 20 minutes, then check to see that potatoes are soft and top is nice and brown. Return to oven if not ready.

A note about anchovies: *My mother says you should use anchovies in brine when making this dish. These can be hard to find in the States. You can substitute salt-packed anchovies, although you have to soak and fillet them yourself. If you end up with anchovies packed in oil, the most common variety, use only 10 fillets, and rinse and dry them well.*

Quickly Pickled Turnips

Pickled turnips are popular in many parts of the world. This recipe is simple and does not involve any major canning projects.

MAKES APPROXIMATELY **1** CUP OF PICKLES

3/4 cup water

1/3 cup cider vinegar

1 tsp salt

1 Tbsp honey

2 cloves garlic, peeled and left whole

1/2 tsp whole peppercorns

1/2 tsp whole coriander seeds

1/2 tsp whole mustard seeds

6 small turnips, scrubbed, ends trimmed, unpeeled, and cut into 1/4-inch slices

Combine water, vinegar, salt, and honey in a small saucepan. Bring to a boil, then remove from heat, stirring to be sure salt has fully dissolved. Add garlic, peppercorns, coriander, and mustard. Let cool for 15 minutes.

Place turnips in a medium bowl and pour the brine over them. Cover and refrigerate for a couple of hours, mixing occasionally to be sure all the vegetables get covered. Serve turnips as a side dish, or use in salads or sandwiches. These get quite pickle-y after a few days, so eat them up quickly if you like them mild. Take your time if you like them spicy.

Turnips

I avoided turnips for a long time, and used to hope each week that my farm-share box would be turnip-free. I was in error. There are numerous turnip varieties which can all be put to excellent use. Smaller "baby" turnips (like the hakurei) can be thinly sliced and eaten raw, or quickly stir-fried. Bigger and spicier turnips make great additions to stock, mashed potatoes, stews, and pot roasts. And the spicy greens can substitute for kale in most recipes.

Matzo Ball Soup

Matzo ball soup usually has homemade chicken soup as its base. This recipe relies on root vegetables for flavor. It's a good substitute for people without the time to make homemade chicken stock, or for vegetarians. You can use any favorite dumpling, not just matzo balls. I find matzo balls are much better when cooked separately as opposed to directly in the broth, whereas other dumplings are fine cooked straight in the broth.

SERVES 6

For the matzo balls

5 eggs

2 Tbsp safflower or grapeseed oil

1 tsp salt

1/2 tsp pepper

2 Tbsp water

1 cup matzo meal

For the broth

2 Tbsp olive oil

6 cloves garlic, chopped

1 leek, washed and chopped

1 small onion, unpeeled and quartered

5 medium turnips, chopped

2 parsnips, peeled and chopped

Matzo balls

Whisk eggs, oil, salt, pepper, and water in a medium bowl. Beat well; yolks and whites should be completely blended. Add matzo meal and stir. The mixture should be completely integrated. If it seems loose, add an extra tablespoon matzo meal. It will thicken a bit as it rests. Refrigerate while you make the broth.

Broth

Heat the oil in a large saucepan over medium heat. Add garlic, leek, onion, turnips, parsnips, potatoes, sugar, and 1/2 teaspoon salt and cook, stirring regularly, until vegetables have begun to brown, about 10 minutes. Add tomato paste to pan and cook, stirring constantly, for 1 minute. Add wine and scrape up browned bits from bottom of pan. Cook off wine for several minutes, until almost gone. Add bay leaves, water, soy sauce, and peppercorns, and bring to a boil.

Reduce heat and simmer, uncovered, for 30 minutes (or 45, if you have the time). Do not adjust salt while cooking; the broth is reducing, and will get saltier as it simmers. Strain into a medium saucepan, or into a storage container if you are refrigerating the broth for later. You should have between 6 and 7 cups of broth. Adjust for salt and pepper.

While broth simmers, bring a large pot of salted water to a boil. Form the matzo ball mixture into balls about 1 1/2 inches in diameter. You will end up with about thirty. Don't fuss too much with them, as they don't have to be perfectly round. Moistening your fingers may make it easier to shape them. Carefully drop them into the rapidly boiling water. When water returns to a boil, lower the flame to low and cover the pot. Simmer, covered, for 25 minutes, until matzo balls are cooked

2 potatoes, scrubbed, unpeeled, and chopped

1 tsp sugar

salt

2 Tbsp tomato paste

1 cup white wine or vermouth

2 bay leaves

8 cups water

2 Tbsp soy sauce

1 tsp whole black peppercorns

3 carrots, sliced into 1/4-inch-thick coins

sprigs of fresh dill

through. Definitely test one to be sure; it should be puffy and soft all the way through. If the interior is dense, continue cooking.

Remove the matzo balls from the pot with a slotted spoon and drain in a colander. If you are going to refrigerate them for later, let them cool completely before storing. Otherwise, transfer from the colander to a plate and let rest at room temperature before finishing the soup.

To finish the soup, bring strained stock to a simmer. Add carrots and cook until tender, about 30 minutes. Add matzo balls and cook a few minutes, until warmed through. Ladle a couple of matzo balls into each bowl along with the broth, and top with a few sprigs of dill.

"Russian" Italian Salad

For reasons which are unclear, Italians make a version of a mayonnaise-based potato salad that they refer to as insalata russa, *or "Russian salad," but which Russians claim has nothing to do with them. (It is rumored that Russians call it "Italian salad," but that might be some kind of Internet joke.) I don't think the version here is traditional in either Italy or Russia, but it's kind of fun to eat potato salad in the winter. Sometimes this salad includes tuna or chunks of meat, but I prefer it without.*

SERVES 6 AS A SIDE DISH

3 medium turnips, peeled, scrubbed, and cut into 3/4-inch cubes

3 potatoes, peeled, with two cut into 3/4-inch cubes and one potato cut in half

1 cup frozen green peas (thawed or frozen)

2 Tbsp rice wine vinegar

1 Tbsp extra virgin olive oil

1/4 cup mayonnaise

1 Tbsp capers, drained

2 tsp lemon juice

1/2 tsp lemon zest

1/2 tsp salt

1/4 tsp pepper

pinch sugar

pinch ground cloves

2 carrots, cut into 1/2-inch dice

1/2 cup chopped Kalamata olives

3 eggs, hard-boiled and peeled

Bring a medium saucepan of salted water to boil. Boil turnips with the halved potato for about 5 minutes, until turnips are tender. Pour into a colander and run some cold water over them to stop the cooking. Drain well. Discard the halved potato (its purpose is to absorb any bitterness) and spread the turnips out on a sheet pan to let them air-dry a bit.

Bring a new batch of salted water to boil, and cook cubed potatoes until tender, about 7 minutes. Again drain in the colander, but do not run cold water over them. Put hot potatoes and drained turnips into a medium serving bowl. Add peas. Pour vinegar and oil over and stir to combine. Let sit while you prepare dressing.

Whisk mayonnaise with the capers, lemon juice, zest, salt, pepper, sugar, and cloves. Add carrots and olives to bowl with vegetables, pour dressing over, and toss to coat. Adjust seasonings to taste. Place wedges of hard-boiled eggs around the side of the salad before serving. Refrigerate if not eating within the next hour. Bring to room temperature before serving.

carrots

maple syrup

March

flour

onions

March

FEATURED
INGREDIENTS

Carrots,
Maple Syrup,
Onions,
Whole Wheat Flour

MARCH MAY INCLUDE the first day of spring, but in New England, winter produce still dominates. Looking to the future, enterprising farmers will be out planting hardy spring crops like broccoli, peas, and radishes, as well as starting seedlings in cold frames and greenhouses. But at the farmer's market you will mostly find storage vegetables and pantry staples.

There is one special harvest this time of year: maple syrup. Below-freezing nights and above-freezing days create just the right change in pressure needed to move the sap up the maples, making this the best month to tap trees. In Maine, the fourth Sunday of the month is known as "Maple Sunday." Locals head out to their favorite farm for a pancake breakfast, maple ice cream, and a tour of the sugar shack.

If you buy directly from the farm, you can procure a gallon of real maple syrup for under $50. That may sound like a lot of money, but a gallon will last a year, even with regular pancake consumption. It's well worth it. Once you open your gallon jug, pour a pint into a syrup jar and leave that available in the refrigerator. Store the rest tightly sealed in your freezer and refill your jar as needed. It's so sugary it doesn't freeze solid, so thawing time is minimal.

Pasta with Shredded Carrots, Bacon, and Cream Sauce

Combining pasta with carrots seems a bit outlandish, but the carrots' sweetness makes for a nice cold-weather pasta dish. Children especially seem to enjoy this.

SERVES **4**

4 oz bacon, diced

1/4 cup water

3 cups shredded carrots
(from about 3 large carrots)

2 garlic cloves, minced

1/2 cup white wine

1 cup heavy cream, divided

salt and pepper

12 oz spaghetti or other pasta

1 Tbsp butter or olive oil

1/4 cup chopped parsley,
if available

1 Tbsp lemon juice

1/2 cup grated Parmesan
cheese, plus more to serve

Place bacon and water in a medium-size skillet over high heat. When water boils, reduce heat to medium and let water cook off until gone. Finish cooking bacon until it's crisp, but not charred. You may need to lower the heat. Pour off bacon fat so that only a tablespoon remains, leaving the bacon in the pan. Reduce heat to medium-low.

Add carrots with a pinch of salt to the skillet and cook for 3 minutes, stirring once or twice. Add the garlic and sauté for 30 seconds, stirring constantly. Add the wine and simmer for 5 minutes, until it's mostly evaporated. Add 3/4 cup cream to the pan and simmer gently, on low, for 5 minutes, stirring occasionally and letting the sauce thicken. Season with salt and pepper. Remove from heat.

Meanwhile, cook the pasta in boiling salted water. Before draining, scoop out and reserve a cup of pasta water. When the pasta is barely done, drain and return to cooking pot (but not on the hot burner), mixing in the butter or olive oil to prevent pasta from sticking.

Add the sauce, the remaining cream, and chopped parsley to the pot with the pasta. Stir well to combine. Add pasta water, a tablespoon or so at a time, if you find the sauce too thick. Add lemon juice, to taste, to brighten the flavor. Season with salt and pepper to taste, then toss with grated cheese. Serve with more grated Parmesan on the side.

Carrots

Many American kids have chosen baby-cut carrots as their go-to vegetable. Those bland cylinders are completely one-dimensional in flavor: namely, sweet. Carrots from a farmer's market are a completely different affair, coming in many shapes and sizes, and even colors, with a real flavor to them. Carrots are delicious roasted, when they can get almost crispy. Traditional boiling leaves them limp and watery. No matter what color your carrots are, you can use them interchangeably in these recipes.

Beef Stew with Root Vegetables

Everybody loves stews in the winter. They are comforting and filling, and finicky eaters can eat the chunks of things they like, leaving the rest. For the cook, stews are forgiving and not particularly refined. If you follow the basic steps of browning the meat, adding flavorings, and then cooking slowly in a covered pot, you're going to have a good stew. You can increase or decrease the quantities of just about anything in this recipe according to what you like and what you have on hand. For instance, my kids aren't that fond of onions, so I tend to put less onion and more garlic into my stews. But feel free to go onion-crazy if that's your preference.

SERVES **6**

2- to 3-lb boneless beef chuck, trimmed of fat

salt and pepper

1 to 2 Tbsp safflower oil (or other neutral oil)

1 large onion, diced

3 to 4 cloves of garlic, smashed

1 tsp dried rosemary (or thyme or marjoram if you prefer)

1 tsp brown sugar

2 Tbsp tomato paste

1 cup red wine or beer

2 cups water

2 bay leaves

1 1/2 cups turnips, cut into 1-inch dice

1 1/2 cups carrots, cut into 1-inch dice

Pat the beef dry with paper towels and cut away major pieces of fat. Cut into cubes; I like mine large, about 2 inches per side. Season meat generously with salt and pepper. Heat oil over medium heat in large Dutch oven or other ovenproof cooking pot with a tight-fitting lid. (You will need the lid later.) When oil is hot, add one-third to one-half of the beef cubes to the pot. Do not crowd and do not stir—they brown best this way. You should smell the meat browning. If you don't, increase the heat, but don't let it burn.

After the meat is brown on one side, stir the cubes once, and let them brown on another side for a few minutes. Use a slotted spoon to remove meat from the pot to a bowl or large plate. If necessary, pour off some fat so you are left with just 1 tablespoon. Then brown the remaining beef cubes. If at any point the bottom of the pot begins to look too dark, add a spoonful of water and scrape any brown bits off the bottom with a metal spatula.

While the first batch of meat is browning, adjust oven racks so that the cooking pot with its lid on will fit in the oven on one of the lower racks (but preferably not the very bottom slot).

Preheat oven to 300 degrees.

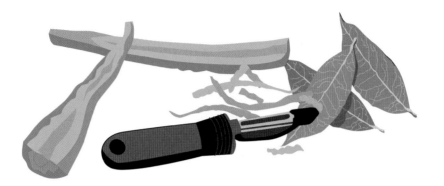

1 1/2 cups parsnips,
cut into 1-inch dice

1 cup frozen green peas

1 to 2 Tbsp sherry vinegar or
cider vinegar, to taste

chopped fresh parsley,
for garnish (optional)

When the last batch of beef is browned, remove it. Keep a tablespoon of oil in the pan. If there's more, pour it off; if less, add some. Turn heat to medium-low. Add the onion and cook about 5 minutes, until softened and browning at the edges. Add garlic, rosemary, sugar, and tomato paste. Let it all sizzle, without stirring, until fragrant, about 30 seconds. Stir for another 30 seconds or so, until tomato paste starts to brown. Pour in red wine and stir well to incorporate all the seasonings and any bits on the bottom of the pot. Let the liquid come to a boil. Simmer 5 minutes. Add the water, beef, and bay leaves, and bring to a boil. Cover pot and place in oven.

After an hour, remove the pot from the oven. (Remember to use a pot holder to remove the lid!) Add the root vegetables and stir the stew. Check the liquid level; if stew looks dry, add a little water. Replace lid (remember that pot holder!) and cook another hour. Check the tenderness of the meat and vegetables. If everything is tender, proceed to next step. If not, return to oven for another 30 or 45 minutes, again adding some water if the stew looks dry.

When meat and vegetables are tender, remove pot from oven and add peas. They will thaw and cook with the heat of the stew. Season with vinegar, salt, and pepper as needed. Thin the stew with water if it is too thick for your taste. Add chopped fresh parsley, if you have some on hand. Serve over noodles or mashed potatoes and rutabaga, or with crusty bread.

Maple Custard Pie

The New York Times *published a version of this recipe in 2006, and it has since made the rounds of the Internet because it's so darn tasty. That version had no starch, only cream and eggs. I thicken it with a bit of cornstarch because I think it holds together better. If you don't have a dark grade of maple syrup in the house, you may want to cook 1 cup of lighter syrup down to the 3/4 cup called for in the recipe, to strengthen the maple flavor, which is pretty subtle otherwise.*

SERVES **8**

1 9-inch pie shell, prebaked (see **Raspberry Yogurt Tart** on page 27 for a tart shell recipe)

3/4 cup maple syrup

1 cup heavy cream

1 cup half-and-half

1/8 tsp salt

4 egg yolks

1 egg

1 Tbsp cornstarch

1 tsp vanilla

1/4 tsp nutmeg

Set a sheet pan in the oven, and preheat the oven to 375 degrees.

In a medium saucepan, heat the maple syrup, cream, half-and-half, and salt. Bring just to a boil, then remove from heat. While the maple mixture is heating, whisk together the egg yolks, egg, and cornstarch in a large, heatproof measuring cup or bowl with a pouring spout. Have a fine-meshed sieve or strainer nearby. When the maple mixture is ready, pour 1/2 cup or so into the yolk mixture, whisking briskly while you add it so as not to cook the eggs. Repeat, half a cup at a time, until you have added about 1 1/2 cups of the maple mixture to the yolks. Then pour remainder of maple mixture into yolks and whisk together. Add vanilla and nutmeg.

Pour the mixture through the sieve into the baked pie shell. Set on preheated sheet pan in oven and bake 10 minutes. Reduce heat to 300 degrees and bake another 45 minutes, until filling is mostly set, but the middle still jiggles. Let cool before attempting to cut. Serve with whipped cream.

Maple Syrup

Although there is an American system of grading maple syrup, many states have their own grades, just to be ornery. The lighter syrups (usually they have one or more A's in their grade) have a finer, more subtle, more lingering flavor. The darker syrups (sometimes called B) are often called for in baking, because their maple flavor is more straightforward. Some people buy one bottle of each and use one for eating straight, and one for baking or cooking. I'm not that organized, but you might be.

Buttermilk Maple Cake

This is one of the first cake recipes I developed for my baking business to incorporate some local ingredients. It doesn't have a super-strong maple flavor, but it definitely has a special taste, as well as an excellent texture. There are no additional spices in this cake so as not to mask the maple flavor. You can make it even more maple-y by serving it with maple whipped cream. Like most Bundt cakes, it keeps very well. If you wrap leftovers tightly, you can enjoy the cake for a week.

SERVES 12

16 Tbsp butter, cut up, at room temperature

2/3 cup light brown sugar

1 1/3 cups sugar

2 1/2 cups all-purpose flour

2 tsp baking powder

1 tsp salt

1/2 cup buttermilk

6 Tbsp maple syrup

4 eggs

1 egg yolk

1 1/2 tsp vanilla

Preheat oven to 350 degrees.

Place butter, sugars, flour, baking powder, and salt into mixing bowl. Beat on low for about 2 minutes. The mixture should look like damp sand, but shouldn't become clumpy. Measure the buttermilk and maple syrup into a 4-cup measuring cup (or medium bowl with pouring spout). Add the eggs, egg yolk, and vanilla to the cup, and whisk well to combine.

Turn the mixer to low, and add one-third of the buttermilk mixture to the flour. Allow it to mix for 30 to 60 seconds, just until combined. Add next third of buttermilk, and do the same. Then add the final third and mix 30 seconds. Stop mixer and scrape down sides. Mix on low another 15 or 30 seconds, until well combined. Mix on medium-high speed about 15 seconds, until batter looks very smooth.

Spray Bundt pan very well with baking spray, and pour in batter. Bake at 350 degrees for 10 minutes, then reduce heat to 325 degrees and bake another 40 minutes before checking for doneness. (To check for doneness, remove from oven and insert a wooden toothpick into cake. It should emerge clean or with only a few crumbs clinging. Also, when you lightly press on the cake's surface with your fingers, it should be springy and firm, not mushy.) Cool in pan on wire rack for 10 minutes, then release from pan and cool completely.

RELEASING CAKES

Many recipe books recommend releasing cakes from their pans after they've cooled for 10 minutes. Sometimes this works for me, and sometimes it doesn't. I have my own method which I picked up from a baker in Portland. After your cake has cooled, heat a couple of inches of water to a simmer in a pot with a diameter larger than the cake pan. Place the cake pan in the hot water, using the steam to remelt the grease which coats the pan. Be careful not to let the water slop over the edges of the cake pan. (If you don't have a large enough pot, just hold the cake over the steam and move it around so every part of the pan heats up.) Keep the cake in the heat for a minute or so at most. Then turn the pan upside down, and tap the edges gently on the counter. The cake should slide freely out; if not, repeat the heating procedure one more time. This method works best if you have applied a lot of grease to your baking pan.

Maple-Glazed Scallops with Carroty Rice Pilaf

Both small bay scallops and large sea scallops are fished in New England. This recipe calls for sea scallops, as they are large enough to easily sear and flip. Bay scallops are best eaten broiled with butter and bread crumbs. They are too small to fuss with pan-frying. (Deep-frying is another story.) This recipe also calls for brown rice. If you prefer white rice, reduce the cooking time by at least 20 minutes, and reduce the water to 1 cup.

SERVES 4 TO 6

For the rice pilaf

3 Tbsp butter

3 cloves garlic, chopped

1 tsp minced fresh ginger

1 1/2 tsp cumin

1 1/2 cups brown rice, medium- or long-grain

1 1/4 tsp salt

3 cups grated carrots (from 3 or 4 medium carrots)

2 1/2 cups water

1/2 tsp pepper

1 1/2 cups green peas, fresh (or frozen and thawed)

For the scallops

1/2 cup maple syrup

1 tsp bourbon

4 tsp cider vinegar or rice wine vinegar

1/2 tsp salt

1/4 tsp pepper

1 1/2 lbs large sea scallops

2 Tbsp butter

Preheat the oven to 375 degrees.

Melt the butter in a medium, ovenproof saucepan with a tight-fitting lid, over medium heat. After butter has melted, add the garlic, ginger, and cumin, and cook for 1 minute, stirring constantly. Add the rice and salt, and cook for 2 minutes, stirring frequently. Add the carrots and stir well to combine. Add water and bring to a boil. Cover pot and place in oven; bake for 45 minutes. Transfer rice into a serving bowl and fold in pepper and peas. Adjust seasonings to taste.

While the rice is in the oven, make the glaze. Mix maple syrup, bourbon, vinegar, and salt and pepper in a small saucepan. Heat over medium heat at a gentle boil, stirring occasionally. When the glaze has thickened to the consistency of honey, remove from heat.

Remove scallops from the refrigerator and pat dry. Heat butter in a large skillet over medium heat. (Do not use a Teflon-coated or nonstick skillet; it will inhibit browning.) When foaming has stopped, place scallops in the skillet with one of the flat sides down. Do not move them. Cook scallops undisturbed on one side for about 4 minutes, for scallops 2 inches in diameter. (Adjust cooking times for smaller or larger scallops.) Once the bottoms have turned a deep golden brown, turn them. If the first one you flip is too pale, leave the others in place for another minute or two. If the crust on the scallops looks burnt, lower the heat.

Once you have flipped all the scallops, add the glaze to the pan. Brush the tops of the scallops with some glaze. Cook without moving for another 3 minutes, continuing to brush the tops with glaze. Remove from skillet.

Serve with rice pilaf on the side, pouring glaze over scallops and over rice if desired. While you're eating, soak the skillet in some water to loosen the sugar and make cleanup faster.

Sausages with Pickled Onions

I'm pretty sure my mother made every single meal we ate growing up, aside from the occasional visit to Mario's for pizza or Peking Garden for Chinese. But in the 1980s my father presciently began subscribing to John Thorne's "Simple Cooking." Thorne, a New Englander, wrote engrossing essays about food in his mimeographed newsletters. He now blogs and writes cookbooks. As a teenager, I came across one issue on my father's desk which discussed, in detail, a "plowman's lunch," composed of bread, cheese, raw onions, and beer. The idea of this meal fascinated me. This recipe reminds me of it, even though it requires cooking meat and the onion is pickled, both of which go against the point of a plowman's lunch. But somehow it feels similar to me.

SERVES **4**, with extra onions left over

2 medium to large red onions, peeled and sliced very thinly

1 cup water

3/4 tsp salt

2 Tbsp honey

1 tsp whole peppercorns

5 whole cloves

3/4 cup cider or rice vinegar

4 of your favorite sausages

Put the onion slices in a medium heatproof bowl. Bring water, salt, honey, peppercorns, and cloves to a boil in a small saucepan. Remove from heat and pour over the onion. Mix well and cover. Let sit for 5 minutes. Pour vinegar over and stir. Cover and chill until ready to serve. (Leftover onions will keep in the refrigerator in a jar for a month.)

Pierce each sausage a couple of times with a fork. Place in a medium skillet, so they aren't too crowded. Add 2 tablespoons of water. Turn heat to medium-high and allow water to cook off. Lower the heat to medium and cook the sausages, turning them as needed, until they are browned all over. If the sausages are very lean, add a teaspoon or two of oil to help them brown.

Serve the sausages with a crusty roll and a pile of pickled onions on the side.

Onions

Onions are one of nature's great achievements. They contribute so much to so many dishes. It's hard to imagine cooking without the flavor base that onions provide. Sometimes in your farm share you may get a lot of onions at once. If you don't feel like storing the onions all winter, these recipes use a few more of them than usual. There are absolute differences between onions—their pungency, sweetness, and crunchiness, to name a few. You can reserve different types for different uses (red onions for salads, for instance, and yellow onions for caramelizing), but they can still be used interchangeably in most recipes.

Mujadara (Lentils and Browned Onions)

Mujadara, *a warming dish from the Middle East, is proof that comfort food transcends geography. Lentils, rice, and fried onions provide a stick-to-your-ribs quality that is comforting to humans in cold weather or times of stress. Some people top each serving with thin onion slices, browned and crisped in a separate pan. (The ones in the dish itself will not be crisp.) It's a nice touch, but not necessary if you don't want to dirty another pan. This is a great winter recipe when you just can't face another bowl of macaroni and cheese.*

SERVES **4** TO **6**

3 Tbsp olive oil

3 large onions, chopped

salt

1 cup whole brown or green lentils

1 1/2 tsp cumin

1/2 tsp smoked paprika

1/2 tsp pepper

1 cup long-grain white rice

1 Tbsp lemon juice

extra virgin olive oil, if desired

yogurt, if desired

Heat olive oil over medium-high heat in a large saucepan or sauté pan, one with a lid. When hot, add the onions and 1 teaspoon salt, stirring well. Cook, stirring often, until onions are thoroughly browned, about 20 minutes. The amount of onions is going to appear crazy, but they will cook down a lot. If they stick to the pan, add a tablespoon or two of water. If they blacken around the edges, lower the heat. When onions are uniformly brown, remove 1/2 cup of them for garnish and remove pan from heat. You are not seeking to caramelize these onions; you want them dark brown.

Meanwhile, partially cook the lentils. Bring 2 cups of water and 1/2 teaspoon salt to boil. Add lentils and simmer, covered, for 15 minutes, enough to par-cook them without making them very soft. Drain away any excess water and reserve lentils.

Return pan with onions to medium-high heat. Add 1/4 cup water, cumin, paprika, pepper, 1/2 teaspoon salt, and rice. Cook, stirring constantly and scraping up the bottom of the pan, for 1 minute. Add 1 3/4 cups water and lentils and bring to a boil. Reduce heat to low, cover, and cook until rice and lentils are cooked through but not mushy, about 15 or 20 minutes. Once or twice during the process, uncover the pan and stir a few times. Check water level; if water is gone before lentils and rice are tender, add 1/4 cup more.

When done, remove from heat and transfer to a large serving bowl, fluffing the mixture as you do to let steam escape. Drizzle with lemon juice and adjust seasonings to taste. Top with the garnishing onions and serve with a drizzle of olive oil or a dollop of thick yogurt.

Steel-Cut Oat Squares

If you have never heard of Richard Sax, that's a shame. He was a cheerful and knowledgeable food writer, whose cookbooks are as fun to read as novels. I adapted this recipe from one in his excellent compendium, Classic Home Desserts. *It is very easy and surprisingly tasty, given the list of ingredients, although I guess the amount of butter is a tip-off.*

MAKES **12** BARS

1 1/2 cups whole wheat flour

1 1/2 cups brown sugar

1 cup steel-cut oats

2 tsp ground ginger

1 1/2 tsp cream of tartar

3/4 tsp baking soda

1/2 tsp salt

20 Tbsp butter, chunked

1 tsp vanilla

Preheat oven to 325 degrees.

Grease a 9 x 13-inch baking pan. Put all dry ingredients (everything except the butter and vanilla) into a food processor. Pulse eight times to combine and cut up oats. Add the butter and vanilla. Process until mixture looks damp and mealy and there are no large chunks of butter left. Press the dough into the prepared pan, trying to keep the thickness even. Bake for 20 minutes. Don't overbake; the squares may seem puffy and loose at first, but will fall and firm up when cooling.

Whole Wheat Flour

For thousands of years, humans have enjoyed biting into a chewy loaf of sourdough bread. Gluten is the substance which provides that chewiness. Unfortunately, whole wheat flour, while being more flavorful and healthful than white flour, has less gluten. This is why it can be tricky to bake solely with whole wheat flour; it provides less structure for baked goods, and makes them feel denser. I grew up on whole wheat bread and I prefer it to white bread, but for baking I usually mix whole wheat and white flour. These recipes seek to capitalize on whole wheat flour's nuttiness and extra flavor, without the density.

Whole Wheat Biscuits

It's a bit tricky to make 100 percent whole wheat biscuits. Biscuits are supposed to be light and fluffy, and whole wheat flour is not known for either of those qualities. If you follow this recipe closely, though, and serve the biscuits warm, they will fit the bill.

MAKES **10** SMALL BISCUITS

2 cups whole wheat flour

1 tsp baking powder

1/2 tsp baking soda

3/4 tsp salt

1/4 tsp sugar

6 Tbsp butter, cold and cut into 1/2-inch chunks

1 to 1 1/2 cups buttermilk

Preheat oven to 450 degrees.

Place the flour, baking powder, baking soda, salt, and sugar in the bowl of a food processor. Whirl briefly to combine. Drop the chunks of butter on top of the dry ingredients, and give about ten 1-second pulses. The mixture should look mealy. If you still see any really large chunks of butter, pulse again a few times, but don't worry too much. (If you don't have a food processor, you can rub the butter into the flour with the tips of your fingers.)

Dump the flour and butter mixture into a large bowl, and pour in about 1 cup of the buttermilk. Stir gently with a wooden spoon or spatula, using a folding motion, until the liquid has all been absorbed. From here, you'll have to make a judgment call about how much more buttermilk to add. You definitely want the dough soft, not dry, but you don't want it sticky—and you absolutely do not want to stir too much. However much you add, stir the additional liquid into the mixture with the same gentle folding motion.

When you are satisfied with the dough's consistency, turn it onto a lightly floured counter. Pat it into a rough rectangle about an inch high, and fold it in two. Do that one more time. Then pat or roll it 1 1/2 inches high, and cut into biscuit shapes using a metal biscuit cutter or a sharp knife. Place on ungreased baking sheets (if you can line them with parchment paper or a silicone baking mat, that's perfect). Put them close together if you like softer biscuits, farther apart if you like crispy biscuits.

Press together scraps from the cutting process, and re-roll or re-pat the dough to cut more biscuits. Even after one re-rolling, the biscuits will be noticeably denser, and a second re-rolling is pushing it. After cutting the second batch of biscuits, I usually just smoosh any scraps together and bake up a couple of biscuit lumps which can be given to impatient children. If you desire, brush the tops of the biscuits with any leftover buttermilk. This will make them a bit prettier.

Bake for 12 minutes, rotate pan, and lower heat to 375 degrees. Bake until browned on top and very fragrant, 4 to 8 more minutes, depending on how done you like them. They are best if served right away, or reheated while wrapped in tin foil, and served warm.

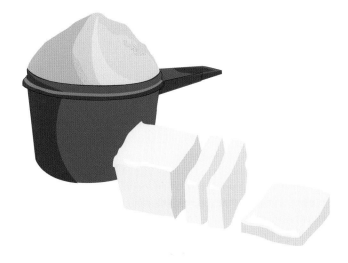

Halfway Healthy Pancakes

My father was the family pancake maker. His favorite recipe involved a lot of sour cream (this one is a little more subdued). But in any case, please remember: Pancakes are "cakes." They are to be "baked" on the griddle, not fried. My father was very clear about that.

MAKES **24** 3-INCH PANCAKES

3/4 cup whole wheat flour

1/2 cup regular flour

1/4 cup rolled oats

1 Tbsp sugar

3/4 tsp baking powder

1/2 tsp baking soda

1/2 tsp salt

1 3/4 cups buttermilk

2 eggs, separated (whites in a medium bowl, yolks in a small bowl)

3 Tbsp butter, melted and cooled slightly

Heat griddle or iron skillet over medium-low heat.

Thoroughly combine flours, oats, sugar, baking powder, baking soda, and salt in a medium bowl. Whisk the buttermilk into the egg whites, and whisk the melted butter into the yolks. Then whisk the yolk mix into the buttermilk. Add all the wet ingredients to the dry ingredients, and stir gently with a rubber spatula until combined.

Spray griddle with cooking spray or brush with a small amount of oil. Use a couple of tablespoons of batter per pancake, depending on how large you want them. Do not crowd the pan because it makes it hard to flip them. I speak from experience. Flip pancakes when the edges are dry and you see a few bubbles, about 2 or 3 minutes. They should be lightly browned; adjust heat if needed.

I shouldn't really need to mention this, but serve with real maple syrup.

SEPARATING EGGS

If you can crack an egg with one hand, you can separate eggs quickly, although it's a bit messy. Hold one hand flat, palm up and fingers slightly apart, over the bowl which will collect the white. I use my left hand for that job. With your other hand, crack the egg against the counter, and then pull it open with your thumb so the contents fall onto the fingers of your flat hand. The white will drip into the bowl while the yolk will stay in your hand. You may have to shake the yolk back and forth a couple of times to loosen all the white. Drop the yolk into its bowl, and repeat as necessary.

The slower but neater method is to crack the egg carefully in the middle. Hold one half of the cracked egg in each hand, with the open sides facing up, over the bowl that will hold the whites. Pass the yolk back and forth between the two halves of the shell, letting the white drip down. Be careful not to nick the yolk with the jagged edge of the broken shell.

April

garlic scapes

chives

fiddleheads

arugula

April

Arugula,
Chives,
Fiddleheads,
Garlic Scapes

WHEN ALL IS RIGHT IN THE WORLD, crocuses and snowdrops pop up in April, and temperatures stay above freezing day and night. Some years, spring is not quite so spring-y, but even during a chilly, muddy April, fresh green vegetables finally arrive at the farmer's market.

Fiddlehead ferns are harvested from the wild in early spring in New England. They are the essence of regional eating. In the United States, fiddleheads are only consumed in the Northeast. In Maine we can even find bins of them at the supermarket.

Another wonderful green this time of year is chives. I love chives because they are so easy to grow, and they pack abundant flavor into a tiny package. It's impossible to kill chives in your yard, even if you aren't much of a gardener. Together with garlic scapes and peppery arugula, they provide a nice, spicy lift to the start of the fresh vegetable season in New England.

Green Goddess Dip 2.0

Green goddess dressing apparently was very popular on the West Coast in the 1920s and '30s. The original versions were pretty light on the "green." I don't think I came across it until I befriended a vegetarian in junior high school. Because of the inclusion of garlic, I doubt this dressing ever made much of an impression in Scandinavia. I'm sure my mother never served it while we were growing up. If you prefer this as a salad dressing rather than a dip, substitute 3/4 cup of buttermilk for the mayonnaise and yogurt, and pour it slowly into the food processor to emulsify.

MAKES **2** CUPS

2 Tbsp extra virgin olive oil

1 Tbsp lemon juice

3 cups torn or chopped arugula or spinach

1 tsp honey

1 garlic clove, minced or pressed

3 anchovies

1/2 cup chopped fresh green herbs (parsley, chives, basil, or a mixture)

1/4 cup mayonnaise

2/3 cup sour cream or Greek yogurt

salt and pepper

Put olive oil, lemon juice, arugula, honey, garlic, anchovies, herbs, and mayonnaise into a food processor or a blender. Blend, scraping down sides, until uniformly green. Place sour cream in a small serving bowl, and stir in puree, combining fully. Adjust seasonings for salt and pepper. Serve with vegetables or crackers as an appetizer.

Arugula

Like most people in the United States, I had no idea what arugula was until the 1990s. I couldn't even wrap my head around what a "peppery" green would taste like, which is how arugula is most often described. Once you taste it, though, you'll know exactly why it's described that way. Even unseasoned, the leaves give a little kick.

Arugula Risotto

This recipe is good for those who really enjoy arugula's spicy kick. The arugula is incorporated in two ways: as a pesto-like puree, and tossed in at the end by itself. The more arugula-ish you want it, the more you can include at the end. To make it less peppery, use the puree only.

SERVES **4** AS A SMALL MAIN COURSE

4 cups vegetable broth or water

3 Tbsp extra virgin olive oil, divided

3 garlic cloves, peeled and lightly smashed

salt

2 cups arborio rice

2 bunches arugula, washed and torn or chopped (about 4 cups), divided

1/4 cup grated Parmesan cheese, plus more for serving

1/4 cup grated pecorino cheese

1/4 cup chopped walnuts

1/2 tsp lemon zest

2 tsp lemon juice

1/2 tsp pepper

1 Tbsp butter

Heat the broth in a small saucepan. Once it boils, turn heat to low and leave the broth on the burner to keep it warm.

Heat 1 tablespoon olive oil in a medium saucepan over medium heat. Add the garlic and 1/2 teaspoon salt and cook for a minute, stirring occasionally, until garlic begins to turn golden. Remove garlic from pan, reserving for later, and add rice. Cook rice for 2 minutes, stirring frequently. Add 2 cups of warm broth and stir vigorously. Bring to a boil. Reduce heat, keeping the mixture simmering modestly. Cook uncovered, stirring regularly and vigorously until the liquid evaporates.

Add the remainder of the broth to the rice one ladleful (about 1/4 cup) at a time. If you run out of broth, add heated water. Each time you add the broth, stir well and wait until the liquid evaporates before adding more. Continue this process until rice is cooked a little bit less than your desired texture. It should be somewhat firm, because it will absorb liquid from the puree.

While the rice is cooking, make the puree. Place 3 cups of the arugula in a food processor and whirl a few times. Scrape down bowl, and add the reserved garlic, the cheeses, walnuts, 1/4 tsp salt, lemon zest and juice, and remaining 2 tablespoons olive oil. Blend to make a puree, scraping down the bowl as needed.

When rice is still somewhat firm, stir in 2 tablespoons of broth, the puree, the pepper, and the remaining cup of chopped arugula. Add the butter, stir to incorporate, then remove from heat, cover, and let the risotto sit a few minutes. Adjust seasonings to taste. Serve with additional Parmesan cheese.

Substantial Arugula Salad

This is a salad with a lot of "treats" or components in it, to keep you poking around for more. It's a good one when there aren't that many fresh vegetables to choose from yet, but you still feel like eating a big bowl of salad.

SERVES 4 AS A MAIN COURSE, 6 TO 8 AS A SIDE DISH

4 slices bread, cut into 3/4-inch cubes (about 2 cups)

salt and pepper

3 Tbsp extra virgin olive oil, divided

1 cup medium-grain bulgur wheat

3 sun-dried tomatoes, finely chopped

2 tsp lemon juice

2/3 cup plain yogurt (Greek, if possible)

3 Tbsp red wine vinegar

1 Tbsp Dijon mustard

1 tsp honey

1/2 tsp lemon zest

1/2 tsp cumin

1/2 tsp dried oregano

2 small to medium heads arugula, washed, dried, and shredded (about 8 cups)

1/2 small red onion, thinly sliced

2 medium carrots, shredded

5 or 6 radishes, thinly sliced

1/2 cup pitted Kalamata or other brined olives

3/4 cup dried cherries

To make the croutons, preheat oven to 375 degrees. Put the bread cubes on a sheet tray, sprinkle with 1/4 teaspoon salt and 1/4 teaspoon pepper, and drizzle with 1 tablespoon olive oil. Toss to combine, then spread the cubes out in a single layer. Toast in the oven for 6 minutes, then stir well, and toast another 5 to 10 minutes, depending on how brown you want them. Cool.

While croutons are toasting, make the bulgur. Put the bulgur, sun-dried tomatoes, and 3/4 teaspoon salt in a medium heatproof bowl. Pour 1 1/2 cups of boiling water over and cover bowl with a pot lid or dinner plate. Let sit for 20 minutes, then check the bulgur's consistency. You want it to be cooked through (not crunchy). Squeeze the lemon juice over the bulgur and fluff it with a fork to release steam. Cool.

For the dressing, whisk together yogurt, vinegar, 2 tablespoons olive oil, mustard, honey, lemon zest, cumin, oregano, and 1/2 tsp salt in a bowl or a cup with a spout.

To assemble the salad, put arugula, onion, carrots, radishes, olives, and cherries in a large salad bowl. Add bulgur and toss to combine. Add croutons and pour dressing over, again tossing well to combine. Adjust for salt, pepper, and acidity, adding more lemon juice if desired.

Chive and Buttermilk Scones

There's no reason all scones must be sweet. This recipe is for savory ones, which go nicely with scrambled eggs. Scones are always best fresh out of the oven, but if you have to reheat them, wrap them in foil and warm them in the oven, not in the microwave.

MAKES **12** SCONES

2 2/3 cups flour

1 cup cornmeal

1 Tbsp plus 1 tsp baking powder

3/4 tsp salt

3/4 tsp baking soda

14 Tbsp butter, cold and cut into chunks

3 1/2 oz cheddar cheese, cold, cut into 1/2-inch chunks (to fill 1 cup)

1 1/2 cups buttermilk

1/2 cup chopped chives (or more if you like)

12 thin slices of cheddar cheese

Preheat oven to 425 degrees.

Place flour, cornmeal, baking powder, salt, and baking soda in the bowl of a food processor. Whirl a few times to combine. Add butter and cheese chunks and pulse ten times, to cut them into small pieces, without making a sticky dough. If you don't have a food processor, you can cut the butter and cheese in with a pastry cutter or your fingers. Don't worry if the cheese remains in pretty large pieces.

Turn mixture into a bowl and pour in buttermilk. Fold a few times, using a wooden spoon or rubber spatula. Add chives, and fold gently until all the liquid is incorporated and the dough is coming together. Don't overmix; it's okay for the dough to be very shaggy.

Turn the dough out of the bowl onto a lightly floured counter. Fold a few times to unify dough. Divide into two halves and pat each half into a disc 1 1/2 inches high. Cut each disc into six triangles and place on a rimmed baking sheet, lined with parchment or a silicone baking mat. Place a slice of cheese on top of each wedge and bake for 15 to 18 minutes, until the scones puff up and become brown on top. Do not overbake.

Chives

Herbs are underutilized in New England cooking. We've long been known for our use of butter and salt as the seasonings of choice. Chives (and garlic scapes) are a good way to improve on this. Chives can be harvested throughout the spring, summer, and fall. Plant a clump outside and snip off a handful every time you need a little oomph in your scrambled eggs or tomato soup, or ask your farmer to bring you a bunch each week.

Carrot, Lemon, and Chive Salad

A college friend made me this salad one night. I was surprised at how good it was, considering it has so few ingredients. It's another nice way to have a salad when there is little fresh produce available.

SERVES **4** TO **6**

6 to 8 medium or large carrots

1 Tbsp extra virgin olive oil

2 Tbsp lemon juice, or more
if you like

1 tsp honey

1/2 cup minced chives

1/2 tsp salt

1/2 tsp pepper

1/2 tsp dried oregano (optional)

Shred the carrots using the large side of a box grater, or the shredding disc of a food processor. Toss in a serving bowl with remaining ingredients.

Scalloped Parsnips and Potatoes with Chives

I remember taking my visiting Norwegian aunt to a Chinese restaurant, where she innocently asked whether she could have boiled potatoes as a substitute for rice. Norwegians really love their boiled potatoes. I do not share that affection. When I was a child, some neighbors from the Midwest served me scalloped potatoes for supper one night. When my mother saw how much I liked potatoes cooked with cream and cheese, she added scalloped potatoes into her menu rotation.

SERVES **6** AS A SIDE DISH

1 1/4 cups half-and-half

4 medium potatoes (about
1 1/2 lbs), peeled and sliced
1/4-inch thick

salt

1 1/2 to 2 cups grated parsnips
(from 3 or 4 medium parsnips)

1/2 tsp pepper

1/2 cup chopped chives, or
more if desired

6 Tbsp heavy cream

1 1/2 cups grated Gruyere,
fontina, or other favorite
melting cheese

Preheat oven to 425 degrees. Butter a shallow 9 x 11-inch casserole dish.

Heat the half-and-half in the microwave or on the stovetop until warm. Do not boil.

Spread potatoes in prepared casserole dish. Sprinkle with 1 teaspoon salt. Pour half-and-half over and cover dish tightly with tin foil. Bake for 20 minutes. Remove from oven and add parsnips, pepper, and chives. Stir well. The dish may not seem moist enough, but the parsnips will release liquid while baking. Cover again with foil and bake 20 minutes.

Remove from oven. Fold mixture several times with a rubber spatula. Check potatoes for doneness; they should be almost fully tender at this point. If they are not, cover dish with foil and return to oven for 10 minutes.

Taste and adjust salt and pepper as needed. Pour cream over the vegetables. Sprinkle cheese on top. Return to oven, uncovered, for 10 or 15 minutes, rotating as needed to brown the entire dish. Let rest a few minutes before serving.

Salads, Soups, and Other Ideas for Fiddleheads

There aren't too many ways to cook fiddleheads. Steaming them for 10 minutes is really the best way; then you can decide what to do with them next. Some ideas are listed below (to call them "recipes" would be stretching it). Just don't pair them with anything too strongly flavored, since their own flavor is subtle. And you never want to cook them for too long.

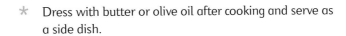

* Dress with butter or olive oil after cooking and serve as a side dish.

* Add vinegar or lemon juice and a handful of chives and serve as a salad.

* Put them, hot, over spinach for a wilted salad, or let them cool and toss them into a green salad.

* Substitute for asparagus in pasta or risotto dishes.

* Sauté with mushrooms and eat with toast.

* Make a soup by cooking the ferns in broth with sautéed onions and adding some cream at the end.

Fiddleheads

Some culinary types feel that fiddleheads get too much attention, given their unremarkable flavor. And there is a bit of intrigue about how to cook the ferns. Although no toxin has been found in the plants, people have reported stomach ailments after eating raw or lightly cooked fiddleheads. Thus, many recipes recommend a long cooking time—say, 20 minutes of boiling. That leaves you with a very mushy green, which is sad, because the best part of the young ferns is their unique texture. When steamed for 10 minutes or so, they are somehow chewy, firm, and tender all at the same time.

Braised Tempeh with Garlic Scapes

Tempeh is a fermented soy product that originated in Indonesia. Mainers are lucky that Lalibela Farm in Bowdoinham makes several delicious varieties of tempeh, so when you need a vegetarian option or a switch from animal protein, there's a great local option.

SERVES **4**

2 Tbsp soy sauce

6 Tbsp ketchup

2 garlic cloves, smashed

1 Tbsp minced fresh ginger

2 tsp toasted sesame oil

1 Tbsp maple syrup

2 Tbsp rice wine vinegar

1/2 tsp hot chili sauce (optional)

1/2 cup water

1 lb tempeh, any variety, cut into 1/3-inch-thick slices

2 Tbsp peanut or canola oil

2 cups roughly chopped garlic scapes

2 cups snow peas, trimmed if necessary

Mix soy sauce, ketchup, garlic, ginger, sesame oil, maple syrup, vinegar, chili sauce, and water in a large skillet. Place on medium-high heat and add tempeh pieces, stirring to coat thoroughly. Bring to a boil, then turn heat to medium-low. Simmer, stirring regularly, for 15 minutes or so, until tempeh has darkened considerably. Sauce will thicken; if surface of pan begins to get too dark, deglaze with a little water and scrape darkened bits off bottom.

Turn heat up to medium. Push tempeh to sides of pan and add peanut oil to middle. Add garlic scapes and cook for a minute, stirring constantly. Add snow peas and stir vegetables and tempeh together. Cook for another minute or two, just until snow peas are bright green and cooked through. Remove to a serving platter and eat over rice or noodles.

Garlic Scapes

If you are new to a New England farmer's market in spring, garlic scapes will probably be one of the first items to confuse you. Unless your parents or grandparents had excellent knowledge of how to give food maximum flavor with maximum frugality, you did not eat garlic scapes growing up. I know I never did. The word scape *just means leafless stem or stalk, and that's all it is: the green part of a garlic bulb which grows aboveground. It tastes just like garlic, only a little less aggressively so, and does well in sautés and stir-fries.*

Pasta with Mushrooms and Garlic Scapes

In the spring, your farmer's market will ideally have some local mushrooms available. They are going to cost more than supermarket mushrooms, but they will also have a lot more flavor. If you wish, you can make this a richer sauce by adding some cream at the end.

SERVES **4**

12 oz campanelle, orecchiette, or other short, curly pasta

1 lb assorted mushrooms

2 Tbsp butter

2 Tbsp olive oil, divided

salt and pepper

1/2 tsp lemon zest

1/4 cup minced parsley

3 cups chopped garlic scapes

2 Tbsp brandy (if you must, you can substitute dry sherry)

1 tsp lemon juice

1/2 cup grated Parmesan cheese, plus more for serving

Cook the pasta in salted water. Reserve a cup of pasta water before draining the pasta.

While pasta is cooking, prepare the mushrooms by wiping them clean and slicing them so they are about 1/4-inch thick. You can rinse them quickly instead, but they should be dry before sautéing. Heat the butter and 1 tablespoon olive oil in a large skillet over medium-high heat. When hot, add mushrooms and cook for about 4 minutes, stirring frequently, until mushrooms have absorbed the fat and the pan looks dry. Keep sautéing and stirring without adding anything to the pan, until the mushrooms begin releasing moisture and start browning. When mushrooms are browned and fragrant, remove the pan from the heat. With a slotted spoon, move the mushrooms from the pan into a serving bowl. Toss them with 1/2 teaspoon salt, 1/2 teaspoon pepper, lemon zest, and parsley.

Return the pan to medium heat and add the remaining tablespoon of olive oil. Add garlic scapes and 1/4 teaspoon salt. Sauté for 3 minutes, stirring often, until scapes are wilted. Add the brandy, stirring to scrape up any bits stuck to the bottom of the pan. When the brandy has mostly cooked off, return the mushrooms to the pan for a minute or two, stirring to reheat and incorporate with the scapes.

Add pasta and lemon juice to skillet and toss to coat thoroughly, heating another minute or so. Pour pasta into serving bowl and adjust for salt and pepper. Toss with the Parmesan cheese and add some of the reserved pasta water if the sauce seems dry.

Garlic Scapes and Potato Soup with Chive Popovers

My kids love soup night. Why? Because it usually means some kind of baked good is served along with the soup. Popovers are a special favorite. I think many kids can be convinced to eat a second helping of soup if they know they'll get a second popover, too. I know I would.

SERVES **4**, with leftover popovers

1 1/4 cups flour

salt

3 eggs

1 1/4 cups milk

1/2 cup minced chives

2 Tbsp butter or olive oil

4 cups roughly chopped garlic scapes, plus some minced for serving

1/4 tsp sugar

4 cups vegetable or chicken broth

1 medium potato, peeled, and cut into 3/4-inch chunks

1 cup cooked white beans (optional)

1 cup chopped or torn arugula

1 cup half-and-half

1/4 tsp pepper

1/4 tsp nutmeg

1 tsp lemon juice

Start by making the popover batter. Combine the flour and 1/2 teaspoon salt in a large measuring cup or a medium bowl with a spout. Beat the eggs and milk together in a small bowl. Pour this into the flour mixture. Whisk well to combine, making sure to incorporate any flour on the bottom. Stir chives in with a rubber spatula.

Preheat oven to 450 degrees. Let batter sit while you make the soup and the oven preheats. You can also make this batter the night before, or in the morning, and let it sit, refrigerated, until you are ready to use. Let it come to room temperature while the oven preheats.

Meanwhile, start the soup. Melt butter in a medium saucepan over medium heat. Add garlic scapes, sugar, and 1/2 teaspoon salt. Sauté for about 4 minutes, stirring frequently, until scapes start wilting. Add broth and potato chunks and bring to a boil. Reduce heat to low and simmer, partially covered, until potatoes and scapes are tender, about 15 minutes.

When the oven has preheated and the popover batter has rested for at least 20 minutes, place an empty muffin tin in the oven for 2 or 3 minutes. Gently stir the popover batter to recombine. Remove tin and spray each depression with a blast of baking spray. Pour the batter into the muffin sections, filling each about one-half to two-thirds full. Place immediately in oven and bake for 15 minutes. Do not open the oven door again.

After 15 minutes, reduce heat to 350 degrees and bake another 10 minutes or so, until popovers are nicely browned and puffed up. When done, remove them immediately from the muffin tin and poke a hole in the bottom of each one to let the steam out.

While popovers are baking, finish the soup. When potatoes are cooked, remove soup from heat. Blend soup in batches in a blender or food processor or with an immersion blender until completely smooth. Return to heat. Add beans (if using), arugula, and half-and-half. Heat through, allowing arugula to wilt. Season with pepper, nutmeg, and lemon juice, adding more salt if needed.

A note about the beans: *They will sink to the bottom of the pot, so scoop from the bottom to give each person a serving.*

May

radishes

rhubarb

lettuces

asian greens

May

Asian Greens, Lettuces, Radishes, Rhubarb

THE WARM WEATHER of May brings a burst of new energy, inspiring us to all kinds of outdoor activities. Lilacs, rhododendrons, and peonies bloom. Gardeners are happy to be out in their yards again. Birds return from their southern vacations, and animals emerge from winter hideaways. Memorial Day approaches, marking the beginning of tourist season and the start to summer.

The farmer's market feels celebratory, too. Outdoor stalls carry many more choices than were available just a few weeks earlier. Some of the delightful hallmarks of the early growing season appear: rhubarb, beloved by many pie eaters; radishes and lettuces, promising fresh, local salads once more; and a host of greens of all shapes and shades, extremely versatile and healthy.

After that long, cold season of storage vegetables, many of us swear off parsnips for the foreseeable future. May is the start of fresh abundance. Let the festivities begin.

Asian Green Salad

A real local salad—finally! Because the word Asian *is in their name, perhaps these greens belong in a salad with Asian overtones. Fortunately, Asia is a pretty big place, so that includes a lot of different flavors. The big question is: Should you put those crazy crispy fried noodles on top, the canned ones from La Choy? I think we'll have to answer that for ourselves.*

SERVES **4**

1 cup chopped, unsalted cashew nuts

6 cups torn tender Asian greens (tatsoi, mizuna, pea shoots)

2 cups lettuce or arugula, or a mixture

2 medium carrots, sliced into coins or matchsticks

5 radishes, thinly sliced

1 cup snow peas, raw or blanched

1 small garlic clove, minced

2 Tbsp vegetable oil

1 Tbsp toasted sesame oil

1 Tbsp lime juice

2 Tbsp plus 1 tsp rice vinegar

1 Tbsp honey

2 tsp soy sauce

1/2 tsp fish sauce

1/2 tsp Asian chili sauce (like sriracha)

1/4 tsp salt

1/2 cup minced chives

If cashews are raw, toast them in a 350-degree oven for about 6 minutes, until fragrant. Set aside to cool, then chop.

Place greens, lettuce, carrots, radishes, and snow peas in a large serving bowl.

To make the dressing, put garlic, oils, lime juice, rice vinegar, honey, soy sauce, fish sauce, chili sauce, and salt in a small bowl and whisk well to combine. (Another method is to put these into a small jar and shake vigorously.) Pour this dressing over salad and toss well to combine. Sprinkle cashews and chives on top and serve.

Asian Greens

The term Asian greens *encompasses a number of green-leafed vegetables commonly used in dishes from East and Southeast Asia. They are easy to grow in the New England climate, and I wonder if one day the word* Asian *will fade from the name, or if, as in the case of the rutabaga (known as a* swede*), the area of origin will stick forever. Some varieties include tatsoi, mizuna, bok choy, and choy sum. These are all in the cabbage family, but you wouldn't necessarily guess it by their taste. They can be stir-fried or used raw as salad greens, if you like a little bite with your salad.*

Rice Noodle Soup with Greens

As with most noodle soups, this does not reheat well, as the noodles become too soft. If you are planning on making it ahead of time, keep the noodles separate. You can usually find five-spice powder, rice noodles, fish sauce, and sriracha in the Asian section of the supermarket.

SERVES **4**

2 Tbsp peanut or canola oil

1 medium onion, thinly sliced

1 Tbsp finely chopped fresh ginger

3 garlic cloves, minced or pressed

1 tsp five-spice powder

3/4 tsp salt

1/2 tsp pepper

6 cups water

1 good-size (10 oz or so) skinless, boneless chicken breast

6 oz rice stick noodles, thin- or medium-size

10 packed cups Asian greens (about 2 medium bunches or half a pound), torn into small pieces

3 Tbsp soy sauce

1 tsp Asian chili sauce (like sriracha), or more if desired

1 Tbsp fish sauce

1 Tbsp rice vinegar

1 to 3 tsp brown sugar, depending on taste

In a large soup pot, heat the oil over medium-high heat. Add the onion slices and cook for 5 minutes, stirring often, until they start to brown. Add ginger, garlic, five-spice powder, salt, and pepper. Stir well. Add water and chicken breast and bring to a boil. Lower to a simmer, cover, and poach breast for 12 minutes.

Remove pot from heat and let it sit, covered, for 10 minutes. Remove chicken to a plate and check internal temperature. It should read 165 degrees at its thickest part. If it doesn't, return chicken to the pot, return pot to a simmer, and cook 5 more minutes.

While chicken is cooking, put rice noodles in a medium heatproof bowl and cover with boiling water. Let noodles sit for 10 minutes, then drain.

While chicken is resting on the plate, add greens, soy sauce, chili sauce, fish sauce, vinegar, and sugar to the pot. Bring to a light simmer and cook for 5 minutes, until greens are nicely wilted. When chicken is cool enough to handle, cut or tear chicken into bite-size pieces. Return chicken to pot and add noodles. Simmer another 2 minutes to heat through. Adjust seasonings to taste.

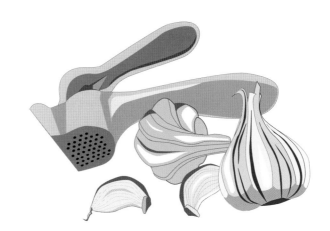

Broiled Tofu with Garlicky Greens

My mother is not a big fan of tofu, and that's putting it mildly. When presented with a dish containing tofu, she carefully extracts each and every scrap from her plate. If you are making this dish for such a person, feel free to substitute some kind of grilled or broiled meat. We're lucky in Maine that we have local tofu available (Heiwa Tofu), and there are also tofu producers in Vermont and Connecticut.

SERVES **4**

1 1/2 lbs firm tofu

3 Tbsp soy sauce

2 Tbsp maple syrup

2 Tbsp rice vinegar

1 Tbsp toasted sesame oil

1/2 tsp Asian chili sauce

3 Tbsp vegetable or peanut oil, divided

1 large bunch or bag of Asian greens (about 12 oz)

1 Tbsp water

4 or 5 cloves garlic, smashed and cut into chunks

Cover a broiler tray with foil. Cut tofu into large slices 1/3-inch thick and lay in a single layer on a few paper towels. Let slices sit for 5 or 10 minutes, so that some of the water is absorbed, while you prepare the other components of the dish.

In a medium bowl, whisk together soy sauce, maple syrup, vinegar, sesame oil, chili sauce, and 1 tablespoon of the vegetable oil. Preheat the broiler.

Chop the greens into 2-inch pieces. If any of the greens you are using have thick stems, cut them in half. Chop the greens roughly. Heat the remaining 2 tablespoons vegetable oil in a large skillet over medium heat. Add the garlic and cook, stirring, for about 30 seconds, until very fragrant but not colored. Add greens and water and cook, stirring often, for about 2 or 3 minutes, until greens are wilting. Add 2 table-spoons of the prepared sauce and cook 1 more minute, still stirring. Remove to a serving dish.

Place the tofu into the bowl with the sauce and turn to coat. Lay tofu pieces on the broiler pan in a single layer, keeping any leftover sauce. Put a little spoonful of sauce on each piece of tofu. Broil tofu for 2 to 4 minutes, until somewhat browned on the edges. Flip pieces over and pour remaining sauce over the tofu. Broil for a final 2 to 3 minutes. The sauce may smoke, but that's okay as long as the tofu itself is not burning. Place on top of greens and serve with rice.

Pea and Lettuce Soup

I don't know that lettuce soup is the first thing that comes to mind for using lettuce, but it's a good way to use your extra greens. Sometimes you're just going to have too much lettuce. This soup is not highly seasoned, to avoid overwhelming the delicate flavor of the lettuce and peas. To make the soup a light main course, add a chopped, hard-boiled egg or sautéed shrimp to each serving.

SERVES **4**

3 Tbsp butter

1 large or 2 small shallots, diced

salt

2 heads Boston or Bibb lettuce, leaves sliced a few inches wide

1/4 tsp sugar

3 cups shelled peas, fresh or frozen, divided

4 cups vegetable or chicken broth, divided

1/4 tsp nutmeg

2 tsp lemon juice

pepper

crème fraîche or Greek yogurt for serving

Melt butter in a large pot over medium heat. Add shallot and 1 teaspoon salt and sauté for a few minutes, until translucent. Add the lettuce leaves, sugar, and 1 cup of peas. Cook, stirring frequently, until lettuce begins wilting, about 4 minutes. Add 3 cups broth. Bring to a simmer, then remove from heat.

Blend soup in batches with a blender or with an immersion blender until very smooth. Return to pot and add remaining cup of broth. Bring to a boil, then lower heat and simmer for 10 minutes. Add remaining 2 cups peas, nutmeg, and lemon juice. Cook for a minute or two—enough time to cook the peas—and then adjust salt and pepper to taste. Serve with a dollop of crème fraîche or Greek yogurt.

Lettuces

Lettuces are wonderful in their variety and their ability to grow quickly in chilly climates. Fresh lettuce from the farmer's market is a heartening sign of spring, and an easy way to incorporate local produce into your meals. There are umpteen types of lettuce, from the supercrispy romaine to the delicate Bibb, from the slightly bitter green leaf to sweet butter lettuce. Pick your favorites and feast away. You should be able to buy one head a week for the entire growing season in most parts of New England. And you ought to.

Lettuce Bundles

A fancy breakfast buffet in Norway could include, among other things, pickled herring, smoked meats, and peppered smoked mackerel, served with hearty whole-grain bread and lots of butter. This may not sound as good as bacon and eggs to you, but you really should give peppered mackerel a try. It's a very festive dish in our house. My mother always has it as an appetizer for the holidays, although not in a lettuce bundle with vegetables as it is here. Nevertheless, this is a good way to try it, even for breakfast. Ducktrap River of Belfast, Maine, makes very nice peppered mackerel.

SERVES **4** AS A SMALL MAIN COURSE

1 cup snow peas, trimmed

6 radishes, trimmed

2 medium carrots, shredded

1/2 cup minced chives or scallions

7 oz smoked peppered mackerel fillets (not canned)

In a small saucepan, bring 2 cups of salted water to boil. Add the snow peas and blanch them for 30 seconds. Remove from heat and use a slotted spoon to move the peas to a colander. Rinse with cold water until cool to the touch. Spread the peas on a clean kitchen towel to dry off.

Put the pot of water back on the stove and return to a boil. Blanch radishes for 30 seconds. Drain in the colander and run cold water over until cool. Pat dry.

Cut snow peas into 1-inch lengths and place in a medium serving bowl. Slice radishes thinly and add to bowl. Add carrots and chives. Pull the skin off the mackerel and discard. Shred fish into rough chunks. Add to bowl.

For the dressing

2 tsp white wine vinegar

1 Tbsp lemon juice

1 Tbsp honey

2 Tbsp Dijon or whole-grain mustard

1/4 tsp powdered mustard

3 Tbsp safflower, grapeseed, or other neutral oil

1/4 cup chopped fresh dill

salt and pepper

1 large head of lettuce (your choice; any kind will work)

Dressing

To make the dressing, put vinegar, lemon juice, honey, prepared mustard, and powdered mustard in a small bowl. Gradually whisk in oil to emulsify, then stir in dill. Pour two-thirds of the dressing over the fish mixture and toss to coat. Let this rest while preparing the lettuce.

Remove core from lettuce and discard, keeping individual leaves intact. Wash the leaves and dry them well in a salad spinner. Tear any very large leaves in half vertically. Place leaves on a serving plate.

When ready to serve, give the mackerel mixture a quick stir. Taste, and add more dressing, and salt and pepper, as needed. Place the lettuce leaves and filling on the serving table. The idea is to take a lettuce leaf, spoon a few tablespoons of the mackerel mixture in the middle, and wrap the lettuce around it. The bundles are meant to be eaten with your fingers. Serve with very dark bread and butter on the side.

Roasted Radishes

Because they have a lot of water, radishes become soft and sweet when roasted, instead of browned. Radishes go very well with butter and salt. Just ask the French.

SERVES 6 AS A SIDE DISH

3 bunches radishes (about 6 cups when removed from their greens), trimmed of greens and scrubbed, halved if larger than 2 inches in diameter

4 Tbsp butter, melted

1 Tbsp olive oil

1 tsp salt

1/2 tsp pepper

1/2 tsp dried rosemary, crushed

lemon, for spritzing

Preheat oven to 400 degrees.

Put radishes in a medium bowl and drizzle with butter and olive oil. Sprinkle with salt, pepper, and rosemary. Toss well, coating completely. Spread radishes and their dressing into a roasting pan. Roast for 20 minutes, until mostly tender and somewhat shriveled.

Put in a serving bowl and spritz with lemon juice. Sprinkle another pinch of salt on top and serve.

Radishes

I grew up thinking there was only one kind of radish—the red one with the white inside—and that it was good for one thing only: dipping into something creamy. As it turns out, there are many types of radishes, and they grow well in cool weather. All of them—red, purple, white, black—are great additions to salads, and it also turns out that many do well when cooked like other root vegetables: roasted, braised, and in soups.

Braised Spring Vegetables

Braising, like roasting, turns radishes soft and sweet. This is a dish best served right away, especially if you include the wilted lettuce. If you are not serving immediately, leave the lettuce out. Wilted lettuce loses its appeal if left sitting too long.

SERVES **4** TO **6** AS A SIDE DISH

2 bunches radishes, with
their greens if possible
(about 20 medium red radishes)

4 to 6 small new potatoes,
scrubbed

3 Tbsp butter

2 small shallots or 1 small onion,
sliced thinly

1 tsp dried thyme

1 tsp salt

1/2 cup chicken broth
(or substitute vegetable broth)

1 Tbsp maple syrup

3 Tbsp balsamic vinegar

4 garlic cloves, smashed

2 cup snap peas

1/2 tsp pepper

1 head lettuce, any kind,
trimmed of bottom end,
cut into 3-inch-wide strips
(optional)

Cut the greens off the radishes (if they are still attached) and discard any tough stems or imperfect leaves. Wash the greens well and dry them. Scrub the radishes and trim the top and bottom. Cut them in half vertically. If larger than 2 inches in diameter, cut into quarters.

Halve or quarter the potatoes to get pieces no larger than 2 inches long.

Melt the butter over medium heat in a large skillet with a lid (or have a sheet pan ready to use as a cover). Add the shallots, thyme, and salt. Cook 2 to 3 minutes, stirring occasionally, until shallots are slightly softened. Place potatoes in the skillet cut side down, and cook for 5 minutes, stirring only two or three times. Add radishes, chicken broth, maple syrup, vinegar, and garlic. Stir to coat vegetables, and bring to a boil. Cover and reduce heat to low. Cook 12 to 15 minutes, until radishes and potatoes are both fully tender.

Remove lid and turn heat to medium-high. Using a slotted spoon, move the radishes and potatoes to a serving platter. Let the liquid boil in the skillet for 7 minutes or so, until reduced by at least half. Add cooked vegetables back to the pan and cook for 2 minutes, stirring regularly. Add radish greens, peas, and pepper and cook for a minute or two. Add lettuce and cook, stirring constantly, for a minute, until lettuce is barely wilted.

Remove from heat and pour vegetables and sauce onto a serving platter. Adjust seasonings to taste. Serve with bread or a cooked grain to soak up the sauce.

Lobster (or Shrimp or Crab) Salad with Radish Slaw

Growing up, lobster at our house was reserved for one occasion: Christmas Eve, served with a white sauce over fish mousse. Now that my family lives in Maine and we want to support the lobster industry, we eat it a little more often. But I've never graduated to cooking the whole crustaceans at home. I just buy the cleaned meat. If you're not feeling up to spending big bucks on lobster, substitute Maine crab or shrimp, or use a medley. You can also use any type of radish you have. The slaw will get pretty moist, because radishes have such a high moisture content. Eat it quickly.

SERVES **4**

3 dozen small red radishes, trimmed and cleaned (about 4 cups, shredded)

1 3/4 tsp salt, divided

3 medium carrots, peeled

2 Tbsp red wine vinegar

7 Tbsp mayonnaise, divided

3 Tbsp lemon juice, divided

2 tsp Dijon mustard, divided

2 tsp honey

1/2 tsp lemon zest

1/2 tsp pepper, divided

1/4 cup minced chives

1 lb cooked lobster meat (from about four 1 1/2-lb whole lobsters), or cooked crab or shrimp meat

1 rib of celery, finely diced

Shred the radishes using the shredding disc of a food processor (or cut the radishes into thin matchsticks). Put prepared radishes into a strainer and sprinkle with 1 teaspoon salt, to draw out some water. Let them sit for 20 to 30 minutes. Meanwhile, shred the carrots with the food processor or the large holes of a box grater.

In a large bowl, whisk together the vinegar, 2 tablespoons mayonnaise, 1 tablespoon lemon juice, 1 teaspoon mustard, honey, lemon zest, 1/2 teaspoon salt, and 1/4 teaspoon pepper. Add the carrots and toss with the vinegar mixture.

To dry the radishes, gently press down on them in the strainer. Turn out onto a clean kitchen towel or paper towels and pat as dry as possible. Add radishes and chives to serving bowl and fold to combine.

In a medium bowl, whisk the remaining 2 tablespoons lemon juice and 1 teaspoon mustard with the remaining 5 tablespoons mayonnaise. Add 1/4 teaspoon salt and 1/4 teaspoon pepper. Chop the lobster meat into large chunks. Add the lobster and celery to the bowl and fold gently to combine. Adjust seasonings to taste.

Serve the dressed seafood on a buttered, toasted bun with slaw on the side, or with some slaw on the sandwich itself. You can also serve the seafood on a bed of arugula or lettuce, with slaw on the side.

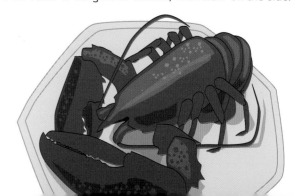

Rhubarb Sauce for Grilled Meat

*Rhubarb cooks down quickly and makes a good, tart base as a sauce for meat. This one goes well with both beef and pork. (For a guide to grilling steak, see the **Grilled Steak with Parsley Sauce** recipe on page 20.)*

MAKES **1** CUP

1 Tbsp olive or other oil

1 shallot or small onion, diced

1/2 tsp salt

1 or 2 rhubarb stalks, cut into 1/4-inch slices to make 2 cups

1/4 cup water

2 Tbsp honey

1 tsp chopped fresh rosemary, or 1/4 tsp dried rosemary

1 tsp Dijon mustard

1 Tbsp lemon juice

1 Tbsp butter

salt and pepper

sugar to taste, if needed

Heat oil over medium heat in a medium skillet. Add shallot and salt and cook 4 to 5 minutes, stirring occasionally, until softened.

Lower heat to medium-low. Add rhubarb, water, honey, and rosemary. Mix to combine. Cook mixture for 8 to 12 minutes. The exact time will depend on how chunky you like your sauce. Cook less for chunkier sauce, more for smoother. Add more water to make sauce thinner, if you desire.

When you have reached the desired consistency, stir in mustard and lemon juice. Remove from heat, and gently mix in butter until melted and thoroughly blended. Season to taste with salt and pepper. If you like a sweeter sauce, add sugar a pinch at a time until you reach the desired sweetness.

Rhubarb

Rhubarb is another harbinger of spring for New Englanders. In April or May, depending how far north you are, rhubarb will suddenly seem ubiquitous. When I was eight, I felt it was a bit of a rip-off to be served rhubarb pie and have it called "dessert" when it was so sour. Of late, I have come to appreciate rhubarb's tartness. When cooked into a sauce with a bit of honey, it makes a great sweet-and-sour condiment. By the way, the color of rhubarb doesn't make any difference to its taste. Some consumers apparently prefer the red variety for its looks. No matter what the color, it's not the most appetizing-looking vegetable when cooked down. So don't bother being too picky about its raw color.

Rhubarb Compote with Oatmeal Lace Cookies

My mother used to cook rhubarb for my father to eat spooned over vanilla ice cream, which he did, practically purring while he did so, he enjoyed it so much. Nobody referred to it as "compote" because nobody referred to anything as "compote" back then. My mom also used to make these excellent oatmeal cookies, although she didn't serve them with rhubarb. I think the crunchiness of the cookies makes for a great pairing with the soft fruit. You can eat the compote as is, or have it over yogurt, sorbet, or ice cream.

MAKES 2 CUPS COMPOTE AND 20 COOKIES

For the compote

3 or 4 rhubarb stalks, cut into 1/4-inch slices to make 4 cups

3/4 cup sugar (or more, or less, to your desired sweetness)

1 Tbsp port

1 Tbsp water

1 Tbsp lemon juice

pinch salt

1/4 tsp vanilla

Compote

Combine all ingredients except vanilla in a medium saucepan. Bring to a boil over medium heat, then cover and simmer 5 minutes. Uncover and simmer another 10 minutes, stirring occasionally. The rhubarb should be completely soft by now. Remove from heat and add vanilla. Cool, then chill. (Chilling will help it thicken.) You can serve it cold, but it's nicer warmed up, at least to room temperature.

Cookies

Preheat oven to 375 degrees.

Spread oats on a sheet pan, and toast 8 minutes, until fragrant but not browned. In a small saucepan, melt the butter. Stir oats into melted butter and let stand for 5 minutes.

In a mixing bowl, beat egg and sugar for minute, until very light. Add in oat and butter mixture and combine well. Stir in remaining ingredients.

Line a baking sheet with parchment paper or a silicone baking mat. These cookies spread out a lot, so each sheet will hold only six, and they need to be widely spaced. Spoon out a tablespoon or so of batter and flatten into a circle. Bake 8 to 10 minutes, until bubbling and brown.

For the cookies

1 1/2 cups rolled oats

8 Tbsp butter

1 egg

1 scant cup sugar

1/2 tsp salt

1 Tbsp flour

1/4 tsp baking powder

1/4 tsp cinnamon

1/4 tsp cardamom

1/2 tsp vanilla

Let the cookies rest on sheet pans for 3 minutes; then use a metal spatula to remove them to a cooling rack. If desired, carefully drape the still-pliable cookies over the handle of a wooden spoon or broom to create a folded shape (prop the spoons or brooms up to make the handles lie parallel to the counter). The cookies will harden quickly. Store in airtight tins to keep them crisp.

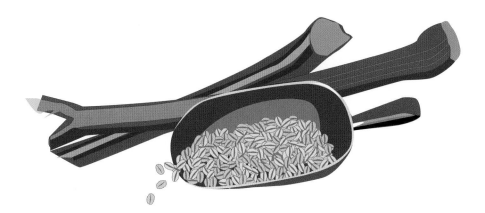

Rhubarb Clafoutis

A clafoutis is a simple French dessert. It's easier than a cake or a custard, and the consistency is somewhere between the two. It can be made with just about any kind of fruit that softens during a relatively short bake. I wouldn't recommend apples, but cherries, plums, and berries are all good. In this case, the rhubarb develops a nice chewy consistency instead of turning mushy. Since there are eggs and fruit involved, clafoutis could be a good breakfast dish and not just a dessert.

SERVES **6** TO **8**

3 or 4 rhubarb stalks, cut into 1/4-inch slices to make 4 cups

3/4 cup sugar, divided

salt

6 Tbsp all-purpose flour

3 large eggs

1 egg yolk

1/2 cup cream

1 cup whole milk

1 Tbsp brandy

1 tsp vanilla

1 tsp lemon zest

Preheat oven to 375 degrees. Butter a shallow 1 1/2-quart baking dish.

Put rhubarb in a medium bowl and toss with 1/4 cup sugar and pinch of salt. Make sure the rhubarb slices are well coated with the sugar, and let sit while you prepare the remainder of the dish.

Mix flour, remaining 1/2 cup sugar, and 1/4 teaspoon salt in a small bowl.

In a large mixing bowl, whisk eggs and yolk together until frothy. Whisk in flour/sugar mixture until well combined. Stir in cream, milk, brandy, vanilla, and lemon zest.

Pour rhubarb into a strainer to get rid of any water which has accumulated. Scatter drained rhubarb over bottom of prepared baking dish. Pour batter over the fruit. Bake for 35 minutes, until puffy and lightly browned. Cool to room temperature.

If desired, dust with powdered sugar. Serve either at room temperature or slightly warmed.

June

peas

kale

sunchokes

asparagus

June

FEATURED
INGREDIENTS
Asparagus,
Kale,
Peas,
Sunchokes
(Jerusalem Artichokes)

ALL KINDS OF LOCAL PRODUCE now arrives each week, from the short-lived, such as asparagus, to the omnipresent kale. Although we may be drawn to the beach, the mountains, or the baseball field, the great variety of fresh food on our doorstep inspires us to be in the kitchen at least for a little bit.

Local strawberries ripen in June. Berries trucked across the country from California or Florida taste nothing like locally grown fresh fruit. They are a fleeting pleasure, however, and sometimes hotly fought over. Arrive late to the market and you may well be disappointed to find every last cardboard pint or quart long gone. Many folks head to farms for an annual pick-your-own ritual.

Unlike blueberries, strawberries have a short shelf life. They also don't fare well when cooked, due to their water content (higher than other berries) and more fragile structure, which makes them collapse when heated. Instead of mixed into baked goods, where they may leave an air pocket, they work best layered on top of previously prepared items, be it pastry cream or lemon curd. It's no wonder that strawberry shortcake, a biscuit topped with fresh fruit, is the season's signature dish.

When you are lucky enough to get a large number of local strawberries, the best bet is to eat them right away. They are wonderful cut up onto cereal, added to salads, or dipped into yogurt. But they also make excellent jam and freeze beautifully. Prepare them now, and in fall and winter you can treat yourself to a strawberry smoothie or strawberry yogurt with real local flavor.

Pasta with Asparagus and Sunchokes

Although the two make a nice combination, if you are missing either asparagus or sunchokes, you can still make this dish. Just double the amount of the vegetable you do have.

SERVES **4**

2 medium sunchokes, scrubbed very well

2 Tbsp plus 1 tsp lemon juice, divided

1 bunch asparagus

2 Tbsp butter

1 Tbsp olive oil

1/2 tsp salt

1 lb fresh tagliatelle, or 12 oz dried pasta such as farfalle or rotini

2 Tbsp balsamic vinegar

1 tsp brown sugar

2/3 cup fresh soft goat cheese (about 4 oz), crumbled

1/2 cup grated Parmesan cheese

1/2 tsp pepper

Bring a medium pot of salted water to boil. Make sure the sunchokes are well scrubbed. Due to their shape, they are impossible to peel easily. The peel is not offensive, but if you can, remove any parts that look particularly thick. Cut the chokes into 1/2-inch cubes to make about 2 cups. Add to boiling water with 2 tablespoons lemon juice and boil while you prepare the asparagus. Boil for at least 15 minutes (20 would be better).

Bring a large pot of salted water to boil. Trim the bottoms of the asparagus and gently peel a few inches more, if they appear tough. Add the asparagus spears to the boiling water and cook for around 5 minutes, until somewhat tender but still a bit crisp. The time will be shorter if the spears are thin, longer if thick. Remove the asparagus with a slotted spoon, leaving the water in the pot to cook the pasta.

Melt butter and olive oil in a large skillet over medium-high heat. Drain the cooked sunchokes and add to skillet with salt. Cook, stirring occasionally, for 5 minutes. Cut asparagus spears into 2-inch lengths and add them with the remaining teaspoon lemon juice to the skillet with the sunchokes, stirring occasionally.

Add pasta to the pot of boiling water (left over from cooking the asparagus) and cook until done—just a few minutes for fresh pasta, longer for dried. Immediately after putting pasta in the water, add the vinegar and brown sugar to the skillet. When pasta is done, drain and turn into the skillet. Stir well to coat pasta with sauce, then mix in vegetables. Turn the pasta and vegetables into a large serving bowl. Add goat cheese, Parmesan cheese, and pepper. Stir to combine. Adjust seasonings to taste.

Asparagus

There isn't much asparagus grown in northern New England, sadly. You'd be lucky to get it in your farm share; more likely you'll be paying a respectable price for a bunch at the market. It's understandable. Asparagus is a perennial which takes time to get established, so it's not a crop farmers turn a quick profit on. In much of New England, you'll probably see asparagus at the market in May, so you may be able to serve it at Passover or Easter. In Maine we often have to wait until June, so we enjoy it on Father's Day.

Asparagus Salad, Niçoise Style

My husband Mark loves Niçoise salad, and this love has proved contagious. It turns out that most people get a kick out of a big plate of prepared, well-dressed vegetables which you can mix and match to your liking. You don't have to wait until tomatoes, green beans, and cucumbers are in season to make such a salad. Use the concept with whatever is at hand. Asparagus is a particular favorite.

SERVES 6 TO 8

7 eggs

2 bunches asparagus

10 to 12 small new potatoes (they should be small and thin-skinned), scrubbed and left unpeeled

1 1/4 tsp salt, divided

1/4 cup white wine vinegar, divided

1 cup extra virgin olive oil, divided

2 to 3 Tbsp minced chives

1/4 cup shallot or onions, minced

1/4 cup lemon juice

2 Tbsp Dijon mustard

1/2 tsp dried oregano
(or 1 Tbsp fresh, minced)

1/4 tsp dried thyme
(or 2 tsp fresh, minced)

1/4 tsp pepper

To hard-boil eggs, place them in a saucepan and cover with cold water. Bring to a boil over high heat, uncovered. When water reaches a rolling boil, remove pot from heat and cover. Set a timer for 11 minutes. When timer sounds, drain the eggs and run under cold water to stop the cooking process. Let eggs cool while you prepare the rest of the salad.

Prepare the asparagus by using the same method as in the **Asparagus Farro Salad** recipe on page 134. Don't cut them into pieces.

Cut in half any potato with a diameter greater than 2 inches. Put the potatoes in a pot and cover with water by an inch. Add 1 teaspoon of salt and bring to a boil. Cook until the potatoes are tender, about 12 minutes. Drain well. Put in a medium bowl. Drizzle with 1 tablespoon of the vinegar and 1 tablespoon of the olive oil. Sprinkle chives on top and toss gently.

Peel one of the hard-boiled eggs. Place the yolk in a large bowl and mash it with a fork or the back of a spoon. Discard (or eat) the egg white. Add shallot, lemon juice, remaining vinegar, mustard, oregano, thyme, 1/4 teaspoon salt, pepper, and finely chopped anchovies. Take 1/4 cup of the olives and chop them finely, and add to bowl. Slowly whisk in remaining olive oil to emulsify. Pour 3 tablespoons of this dressing over the warm potatoes and toss gently to coat.

Bring a medium pot of salted water to boil. Add peas and cook 1 minute; drain and run cold water over them to stop the cooking. Dry on a towel or in a salad spinner.

12 anchovy fillets, drained, rinsed, and patted dry, divided as follows: 2 to 4 finely chopped, 8 to 10 left whole

3/4 cup pitted Niçoise olives, divided

2 cups snap peas

1 or 2 bunches of arugula or other sturdy green, to cover the serving platter

2 4-oz cans good-quality tuna, packed in olive oil, drained

To dress and assemble the salad, arrange the arugula as the bottom layer on a large serving platter. Put peas in the large bowl with the dressing and toss to coat. Remove with a slotted spoon, leaving behind excess dressing. Place peas in a mound on the platter. Place asparagus spears in a mound on the platter and drizzle 3 or 4 tablespoons of dressing over. Make a separate mound of the potatoes. Place the tuna on the platter and separate it gently with a fork. Pour 2 tablespoons of dressing over the tuna. Add olives to the platter in a little pile. Peel the remaining six eggs and cut them into wedges. Arrange them around the platter. Drape the whole anchovies around the platter. Let each person take some of each ingredient onto his or her plate. Provide any extra dressing in a small jug at the table. Serve with good bread.

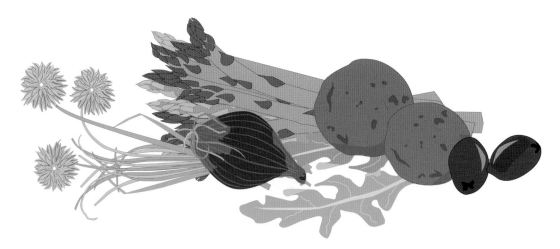

Asparagus Farro Salad

Farro is a type of wheat which is unfamiliar to most Americans. In Italy it is considered poor people's food, whereas here in the States, it is served in fancy restaurants. It has a nice, chewy consistency which makes it ideal for grain salads. If you can't find farro, you can substitute pearled barley instead. Farro can be confusing because it comes in different forms: unpearled, semi-pearled, and pearled, among others. They can be used interchangeably, but I find the semi-pearled easiest to cook with. The unpearled needs an overnight soaking before cooking.

SERVES **4** TO **6**

1 1/4 cups semi-pearled farro

1/3 cup plus 1 Tbsp extra virgin olive oil

4 to 6 large kale leaves, washed

2 Tbsp lemon juice, divided

2 tsp salt, divided

2 bunches asparagus, trimmed of tough ends

1 shallot or small onion, finely chopped

1 garlic clove, minced

2 Tbsp balsamic vinegar

1/2 tsp powdered mustard

1/2 tsp honey

1/2 tsp pepper

1/2 cup coarsely chopped dried apricots

1 cup crumbled feta cheese

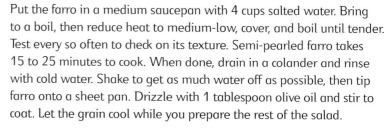

Put the farro in a medium saucepan with 4 cups salted water. Bring to a boil, then reduce heat to medium-low, cover, and boil until tender. Test every so often to check on its texture. Semi-pearled farro takes 15 to 25 minutes to cook. When done, drain in a colander and rinse with cold water. Shake to get as much water off as possible, then tip farro onto a sheet pan. Drizzle with 1 tablespoon olive oil and stir to coat. Let the grain cool while you prepare the rest of the salad.

Fold kale leaves in half and cut out center stems. Cut the leaves in half lengthwise and then slice thinly (1/8- to 1/4-inch wide) crosswise. Put the kale shreds in a large serving bowl. Add 1 tablespoon lemon juice and 1/2 teaspoon salt. With your hands, gently "massage" the lemon juice into the kale for 30 seconds or so. You want to gently bruise but not crush the kale, to make it more tender.

Bring 4 cups of water to boil. If asparagus stalks are particularly large, lightly peel the bottom 2 or 3 inches of the stalks to rid them of anything too fibrous. Lay the asparagus with minimal overlap in a 9 x 13-inch metal baking pan. Sprinkle with 1 teaspoon salt. When water boils, pour it over the asparagus and set a timer. Depending on how thick your stalks are and how crisp you want them, they should sit in the hot water from 4 to 10 minutes. Make sure to test one before draining, to make sure it is as tender as you want. Drain the spears and let them dry on a clean kitchen towel. Cut them into 1- or 2-inch lengths and add to the bowl with the kale.

Put shallot, garlic, vinegar, remaining tablespoon lemon juice, mustard, honey, 1/2 teaspoon salt, and pepper in a small bowl. Whisk these together, then whisk remaining 1/3 cup olive oil into mixture to emulsify. Add farro, apricots, and feta to serving bowl with the kale and asparagus. Pour dressing over, and toss to combine. Let salad sit for 20 minutes to blend flavors, then adjust for salt and pepper before serving.

Sautéed Kale with Vinegar

At some point, sautéed kale became a staple at our dinner table, and kale shows up as a side dish at least once a week. This is mainly because our kids like it, especially the eldest. He actually asks for it as a side dish on his birthday (the main dish being hot dogs). Margaret Hathaway of Ten Apple Farm, author of Portland, Maine Chef's Table, *gave me this recipe. It's particularly good.*

SERVES **4** TO **6** AS A SIDE DISH

3 Tbsp olive oil

2 anchovy fillets, minced

2 cloves garlic, minced

1 large bunch kale, washed, stemmed, and roughly chopped

1 Tbsp red wine vinegar

1/2 tsp salt

Heat olive oil and anchovies in a large saucepan over medium-high heat. Cook for a couple of minutes, stirring often, until the fish browns and begins to smell nutty. Add garlic and sauté for 1 minute, continuing to stir. Add kale and cook 7 to 10 minutes, stirring occasionally, until greens are fully cooked. Add more oil if kale sticks to pan. Stir in vinegar and salt. Adjust seasonings. If the kale has been through a frost, it may be drier and sweeter, and if so may need more oil and vinegar.

Kale

I worked at a farm stand in high school and sold purple kale plants. I had no idea you could do anything with the stuff other than placing the pots on your front steps for decoration. Now it seems that everybody is extolling the virtues of kale. People are eating it raw, turning it into chips, even juicing it. Kale is actually a great way to eat your greens. It lacks the bite of mustard greens and the oxalic acid of chard, and has more body than spinach while still being flavorful. Personally, I don't juice it, but you go right ahead.

Kale and Chickpea Soup

Caldo verde, the kale soup known in southern New England as "Portuguese penicillin," is a delicious and hearty way to use kale during cold weather, when you're ready to be fortified with potatoes and sausage. My mother sent me a recipe for caldo verde when I was in college, and I remember thinking how unusual it sounded and how tasty it was. This kale soup is lighter and more suited to warm weather. I don't know whether it has the power of penicillin, but hopefully you won't need any in the summer.

SERVES **4** TO **6**

2 Tbsp olive oil

1 medium onion, chopped

1 tsp salt

2 cloves garlic, minced or pressed

1 tsp minced fresh ginger

1/2 tsp dried thyme

1 tsp cumin

1 tsp turmeric

1 tsp smoked paprika

3 cups cooked chickpeas
(**Note:** *If you cook these yourself, keep any leftover cooking liquid to use in place of vegetable broth.*)

1 28-oz can peeled whole plum tomatoes, drained of juice

4 cups vegetable broth

2 bunches kale, stems trimmed, cut into 1/2-inch-wide ribbons

1 Tbsp lemon juice

2 Tbsp minced parsley or chives

1/2 tsp pepper

cooked rice and plain Greek yogurt for serving

Heat olive oil in a large soup pot over medium heat. Add onion and salt and cook, letting onion soften, stirring occasionally, for 5 or 6 minutes. Add garlic, ginger, thyme, cumin, turmeric, and paprika. Cook 2 more minutes, stirring constantly, letting mixture get fragrant. Add chickpeas and stir to coat. Cook for another minute, then add the peeled tomatoes individually, squishing each with your fingers to break it apart. Let tomatoes cook down for 3 minutes. Add broth and bring to a boil.

Simmer uncovered for 15 minutes to let flavors blend. Add kale and simmer another 15 minutes, partially covered, until kale is tender. Stir in lemon juice, parsley, and pepper. Taste for seasonings and adjust as needed.

To serve, place a scoop of warm, cooked rice in the bottom of each bowl and ladle soup over. Add a dollop of yogurt on top, if desired.

Risotto with Kale, Garlic, and Beans

Kale goes well with cannellini beans (the small white ones), but if you'd like more of a contrast with the white arborio rice, use any other kind you like.

SERVES **4** TO **6** AS A SMALL
MAIN COURSE

4 1/2 cups water

1 tsp salt, divided

1 bunch kale, washed, stemmed,
leaves cut in half lengthwise

1 Tbsp butter, divided

1 Tbsp olive oil

10 cloves garlic, peeled and
sliced thinly

1 shallot, diced

1/4 tsp red pepper flakes, or
more if desired

2 cups arborio rice

1/3 cup white wine or vermouth

1 1/2 cups cooked cannellini or
other beans
(**Note:** *if you cook these yourself, keep
any leftover cooking liquid and use it to
cook the kale.*)

1/2 cup grated Parmesan cheese

3/4 cup crumbled feta cheese

1/4 cup heavy cream

1/2 tsp pepper

Bring water with 1/2 teaspoon salt to boil in a medium saucepan. When boiling, add kale and cook for 5 minutes. Remove kale with a slotted spoon and let cool on a plate. When kale is cool enough to handle, pour any excess liquid back into the cooking pot, and chop leaves coarsely. Set aside. Return pot to low heat to keep warm.

Heat butter, olive oil, garlic, and 1/2 teaspoon salt in a medium saucepan over medium-low heat. Cook for several minutes, stirring often, until garlic has softened and is very fragrant. Using a slotted spoon, remove 1 tablespoon of the garlic and reserve in a small dish.

Add shallot and pepper flakes to pan and increase heat to medium. Cook for a few minutes and stir often. Add the rice, and stir to coat. Cook for 2 minutes, stirring frequently. Add wine, bring to a simmer, and cook the rice mixture, again stirring frequently, until the wine is almost gone. Add 2 cups of the warm water (used to cook the kale) and stir vigorously. Bring to a boil. Reduce heat, keeping the mixture simmering at a medium clip. Cook, uncovered, stirring regularly and vigorously until the liquid evaporates. Add the kale and stir well.

Add the remainder of the water to the rice, one ladleful (about 1/4 cup) at a time. Each time you add water, stir well and wait until the liquid evaporates before adding more. Continue this process until rice is cooked to just a little bit less than your desired texture (residual heat will finish cooking it). Total cooking time will be around 20 minutes. Add one last small ladleful of water and remove from heat.

Stir in beans, Parmesan cheese, feta cheese, cream, and pepper. Stir well to incorporate, cover, and let risotto sit a few minutes. Adjust seasonings as desired, and serve with additional Parmesan cheese, if you wish.

Poached Salmon with Peas

*Salmon and peas is a traditional Fourth of July dish in New England. Supposedly this is because by July, the peas were ready and the salmon were running. These days we can often get peas by June, but you can't get wild Atlantic salmon at all anymore. Many people buy farmed Atlantic salmon, but I stick to wild, which means Pacific. Not very local. My mother is a whiz at poaching fish, and she provided the directions here. Sauces to serve with the fish are described in the **Sauce with Poached Salmon** tip on page 139. You might also like to round out your meal with some roasted or boiled new potatoes, another traditional side dish for the Fourth.*

SERVES **4** TO **6**

2 quarts water

2 cubes fish bouillon

bay leaf

10 whole peppercorns

8 sprigs fresh dill

1 small onion, unpeeled and halved

1 Tbsp white vinegar

1/2 tsp sugar

3 lbs salmon, 1-inch-thick steaks with skin and center bone if possible; if fillets, as thick as possible and cut into 4-inch serving-size pieces

lemon slices and sprigs of dill or parsley for garnish

Preheat oven to 225 degrees. Place a large serving platter in the oven to warm up.

In a large pot, bring water to boil with the cubes of fish bouillon, bay leaf, peppercorns, dill, and onion. Reduce to a simmer, add vinegar and sugar, and simmer 10 minutes.

Place salmon pieces carefully in the poaching liquid so as not to break them. Poach for 5 to 9 minutes, uncovered; the exact time will depend on whether you are using steaks with bones (longer) or fillets (shorter),

Peas

Both types of peas at the farmer's market are sweet, delightful signs of spring. The English (or garden or green) pea has a tough pod you must remove before eating. The snap (or sugar snap) pea has an edible pod you can eat. (Snow peas are a variety of snap peas.) All peas at the farmer's market are usually wonderful, but be forewarned: The longer the time between picking and eating, the less sweet they will taste. Because of the time needed to shell them, I don't usually buy English peas more than once or twice per season. They are worth the time if you have it. The recipes here assume you are using snap peas, although you can substitute English peas if you prefer. Shelled English peas only need a very brief cooking time.

4 cups halved snap peas

2 cups shelled English peas

2 Tbsp water

1 Tbsp butter

1/4 tsp salt

2 tsp lemon juice

1/4 tsp pepper

2 Tbsp minced mint or parsley
(optional)

as well as on how thick the fish pieces are. To check for doneness, remove one piece and use a fork to pry apart some layers and get a peek at the interior. You should not see raw-looking flesh. Do not overcook or fish will be dry.

Carefully remove fish from poaching liquid with a large metal spatula. Place pieces on preheated platter. If using steaks, peel off skin and remove bones. This will be easy now that they are cooked. Garnish salmon with lemon slices and sprigs of dill or parsley.

To prepare the peas, put both kinds in a skillet with 2 tablespoons of water. Heat over medium-high until water is steaming and peas are tender but not mushy. This will only take a couple of minutes. Drain and put into a serving bowl; top with butter, salt, lemon juice, pepper, and herbs (if using). Stir to coat. Don't overseason or the fresh peas will be overwhelmed.

SAUCE WITH POACHED SALMON

The traditional sauce for Fourth of July salmon was a white sauce with chopped hard-boiled egg in it. I've never had it that way, and frankly, it sounds a tad on the heavy side. Growing up we did eat finnan haddie (smoked haddock) with a melted butter and hard-boiled egg sauce, and it was delicious. My mother usually serves poached fish with a simple sauce of melted butter, lemon juice, and dill. You can also make a quick remoulade: mayonnaise mixed with lemon juice, mustard, capers and/or chopped pickle, and minced dill, in proportions that suit your taste. Remoulade is handy because you can turn leftover poached salmon into salmon salad, which, when presented on lettuce leaves and surrounded by sliced cucumber or radish, makes a pretty first course for company, or a light lunch for family.

Spring Pea Puree

Fresh peas are kind of like fresh strawberries—it's awfully hard not to just eat them raw, when they are crunchy and sweet. But if you can bring yourself to make and save this puree, you will find it a handy way to add pea flavor to many dishes. Pea puree recipes using frozen peas are all well and good, and recipes may call for strongly flavored additional ingredients, such as garlic or mint or Parmesan cheese. I like to keep this puree very simple, to let the flavor of the peas shine.

MAKES **1 1/2** CUPS

3 cups shelled English peas
(it will take about 3 lbs in the pod
to yield this much)

2 tsp lemon juice

1 tsp butter

salt and pepper

1 Tbsp hot water

1 to 2 Tbsp crème fraîche or
mascarpone cheese

Bring a medium saucepan of salted water to the boil. Add the peas all at once and cook for 60 seconds. Drain and tip into a food processor. Add lemon juice, butter, 1/4 teaspoon salt, and a bit of pepper, and blend until smooth, scraping down the bowl a few times. With blade turning, add 1 tablespoon very hot water and blend until incorporated. Remove from processor and fold in crème fraîche or mascarpone.

Turn spring pea puree into a dip by adding some more crème fraîche or sour cream. The puree also makes a nice final ingredient folded into risotto. You can use it as a spread for sandwiches or bruschetta topped with goat cheese or ham. Or try it mixed with an egg, as a filling for a tart or ravioli, or as a saucy underpinning for grilled scallop or shrimp.

Creamy Sunchoke Soup

*This is not unlike creamy potato soup, but the nuttiness of sunchokes makes it
a bit more interesting.*

SERVES 4

4 to 6 medium sunchokes
(about 1 lb), well-scrubbed

2 Tbsp lemon juice

2 Tbsp butter

1 Tbsp olive oil

2 medium onions, sliced thinly

1/2 tsp salt

2 cloves garlic, smashed

1 medium potato, peeled
and diced

4 cups vegetable broth

1/4 cup cream

2 Tbsp dry sherry

1/2 tsp white pepper

1/4 tsp nutmeg

minced chives or other herb
for garnish

Bring a medium pot of salted water to boil. Sunchokes are too lumpy to bother peeling entirely. Just remove any peel within easy reach or that looks particularly obtrusive. Scrub them well and slice about 1/4-inch thick. Add to boiling water with 2 tablespoons lemon juice and boil for at least 15 minutes.

Meanwhile, melt butter and olive oil in a soup pot over medium-high heat. When foaming has subsided, add onions and salt. Cook, stirring often, until onions start to brown. Lower heat to medium-low and continue cooking, stirring regularly, until onions are completely soft. Add garlic and potato to pot. Drain sunchokes and add them. Stir to coat everything with the butter and oil, then add broth and raise heat, bringing liquid to a boil. Reduce heat to low and simmer, uncovered, for 30 minutes. Potatoes and sunchokes should be very tender.

Remove from heat and puree soup in batches. Return to heat. Add cream, sherry, white pepper, and nutmeg, and heat through. Adjust seasonings to taste. Garnish servings with minced herbs.

Sunchokes (Jerusalem Artichokes)

No, they are not from Jerusalem; they are native to North America. And they are not artichokes. They are exactly what they look like: lumpy tubers. Sunchokes are high in both potassium and iron, and have a nice, nutty taste. The big problem is their long-noted tendency to cause (sorry, there's really no good way to put this) gas. The effect varies greatly from person to person, and may diminish for people who eat sunchokes regularly. Cutting them in chunks and boiling them in lemon water helps a lot, as does roasting them slowly and for as long as possible. I think they're worth it.

Fried Mackerel with Roasted Potatoes and Sunchokes

Americans don't eat much mackerel, which seems a shame. It's considered quite a treat in Norway. Mackerel is good in fishcakes, a common and delicious street food there but virtually unseen here. Personally, I think sidewalk fishcake vendors would do quite well in the cities of coastal New England. This fried mackerel recipe is from my mother, and it's delicious. She advises three things: Make sure the mackerel is fresh and firm; cook the fish with the skin on to increase the flavor; and serve with boiled potatoes. I depart only from the last point and suggest serving roasted sunchokes and potatoes on the side instead.

SERVES **4**

6 medium sunchokes, well-scrubbed, unpeeled, and cut into 1-inch chunks

3 Tbsp olive oil, divided

2 tsp salt, divided

1 tsp pepper, divided

6 medium potatoes, scrubbed, peeled if desired, and cut into 2-inch chunks

1 cup flour

1 1/3 cups sour cream

1/3 cup milk

3 fresh mackerel, filleted, with skin on (6 halves)

2 Tbsp butter, plus more if needed

1/4 cup minced chives

Preheat oven to 300 degrees.

Place sunchoke cubes in roasting pan. Toss with 2 tablespoons olive oil and sprinkle with 1/2 teaspoon salt. Roast for 45 minutes, then increase heat to 350 degrees. Add potatoes, remaining tablespoon of olive oil, 1/2 teaspoon salt, and 1/2 teaspoon pepper to roasting pan, stirring them in with the sunchokes. Continue roasting while you prepare the fish. Potatoes will need about 30 minutes to cook through.

Combine flour, 1 teaspoon salt, and 1/2 teaspoon pepper in broad, shallow bowl or soup plate. Put sour cream in a measuring cup with a spout and whisk in the milk to thin it. Have ready a large, heatproof serving plate.

Pat the fish fillets dry with paper towels and sprinkle flesh side with salt. Heat 2 tablespoons butter in a large skillet over medium-high heat. Dredge the fillets in the flour mixture to coat. Fry fillets without crowding; you may need to work in batches. Fry the fish skin side up, for 4 to 5 minutes. Flip and fry 2 minutes on the other side. On the flesh side, fish should be golden brown. The skin side should curl slightly around the edges. If butter begins to burn, lower heat to medium. Place fried fish on heated serving plate and keep in oven to stay warm, if frying in batches. Continue until all fillets are done.

Use a metal spatula to scrape any browned bits from the bottom of the pan. Return all the mackerel to the skillet. Lower the heat to medium-low. Pour the sour cream mixture over the fish. Sprinkle chives over and bring mixture to a simmer. Turn off heat and simmer, with heat off, for a minute or two. Transfer to serving platter. Serve with the roasted vegetables on the side.

July

blueberries

chard

sour cherries

beets

corn

July

THE HEAT OF JULY calls for main dishes that don't require much time in the kitchen. This is the time of year to eat outside on the patio, with something from the grill. Growing up, we seemed to eat all our July meals outside. Corn on the cob seemed to be part of each meal. That still sounds good. If you *are* willing to turn the oven on, it's a wonderful time for making desserts with the blueberries and sour cherries arriving in the market. Both make outstanding pies, cobblers, cakes, and muffins.

Blueberries are available for weeks. Sour cherries are fragile, and come and go quickly. I am particularly fond of their tartness and often eat them right when I get home from the market, before they spoil. If you prefer, preserve or freeze the fruit. Pull them out when the weather is cooler and you're ready to bake again.

Beets are omnipresent in New England farmer's markets throughout the year. Not only do they mature early, but they can also be planted throughout the spring for later harvests. In proper storage, beets keep for four to five months. If you have a winter CSA share, you may find yourself with lots of them in the cold months. During that time roasting is no problem. I prefer roasted beets to any other preparation, so I'll turn on the oven to prepare them even in summer. Boiling is another option if it's just too hot outside.

Beet and Kale Salad

*If your beets come with greens, sauté them as directed in the **Beet and Feta Flatbread** recipe on page 146. When they are cool, add them to this salad for another contrasting texture. You may substitute arugula for part or all of the kale, but skip the massaging step in that case.*

SERVES **4**

1/2 cup pine nuts

1 ball fresh mozzarella, approx. 6 oz

2 bunches kale, washed and stemmed

3 Tbsp lemon juice

1 Tbsp balsamic vinegar

2 tsp honey

1/2 tsp salt

1/2 tsp pepper

3 Tbsp extra virgin olive oil

2 Tbsp chopped fresh basil

6 cooked beets (roasted or boiled), cut into small wedges

1/2 cup Kalamata olives, pitted

1/2 red onion, sliced thinly

Preheat oven to 350 degrees.

Place pine nuts on a sheet tray and toast for 3 or 4 minutes, until fragrant (or toast in an ungreased skillet over medium heat, stirring frequently, until fragrant). Set aside.

Cut the mozzarella into 3/4-inch pieces. Spread them out on a paper towel to absorb some of the moisture.

Cut the center ribs out of the kale leaves and discard. Slice the leaves horizontally about 1/2-inch wide.

In a large bowl, whisk together the lemon juice, vinegar, honey, salt, pepper, and olive oil. Add kale and use your hands to lightly "massage" the leaves together with the dressing. Let sit for 5 minutes. Add remaining ingredients, including pine nuts and mozzarella, and toss to coat with dressing.

Beets

When I was a child, my grandmother would sometimes offer me a bowl of borscht. Seeing my hesitation to dip in, she'd say, "How about if I put a potato in it?" Frankly, I still don't see how a cold boiled potato enhances the appeal of a cold bowl of beet soup. I now enjoy my borscht with some sour cream. Beets have a sweet side and an oniony side. I prefer the sweet, and the best way to bring that out is by roasting.

Beet and Feta Flatbread

This recipe explains my favorite method for roasting beets. It borrows from famed chef Thomas Keller, who is a culinary genius. Since beets can take a long time to cook, you might want to roast them ahead of time (you can prep the beet greens ahead of time, as well). Bring toppings to room temperature while you shape the dough rounds. You can bake or grill these pizzas. If you plan to grill them, keep the dough circles small, about 8 inches in diameter. Large ones become difficult to remove from the grill with their toppings on. You may want to opt for three or four flatbread circles instead of two.

SERVES 4 TO 6

6 to 8 medium beets with greens (plus additional greens like spinach or chard, if desired)

5 Tbsp extra virgin olive oil, divided, plus more for brushing and drizzling

2 1/2 tsp salt, divided

1/4 cup water

2 Tbsp balsamic vinegar

1/2 tsp pepper

1 ball pizza dough

6 cloves garlic, chopped

1 1/2 cups crumbled feta or soft goat cheese

Additional toppings to taste, such as Kalamata olives, blue cheese, arugula, or caramelized onions

1/4 cup minced fresh basil, plus other fresh herbs if available

Preheat oven to 400 degrees. Line a roasting pan with foil.

Remove the greens from the beets and set aside. Scrub the beets and place in the pan. Toss with 2 tablespoons olive oil and 1 teaspoon salt. Add 1/4 cup of water to the roasting pan and cover tightly with foil. Roast 45 minutes. Check for doneness by inserting a paring knife. It should slip in easily. Return any undercooked beets to oven, again covering tightly with foil. Total roasting time depends on size. Some may take up to 90 minutes. Set beets aside. When cool enough to handle, peel and slice the beets 1/4-inch thick. Halve or quarter the slices, but not too small (there's a risk that they will slide off the flatbread). Put slices in a mixing bowl. Add vinegar, 1 tablespoon olive oil, 1 teaspoon salt, and 1/2 teaspoon pepper. Toss to coat.

If you prefer to boil the beets, trim off the greens, scrub but don't peel the beets, and boil in a pot of water with some salt and a spoonful of white vinegar. How long to cook them will depend on their size. After 30 minutes, check for doneness. A paring knife should slip into the beet without resistance. It is better to err on the side of overcooked. After you have drained and cooled the beets, remove their skins and continue as above.

While the beets are cooling, prepare the rest of the dish. If you are baking your flatbreads, put a pizza stone or sheet pan in the oven. Increase oven temperature to 500 degrees. If you are grilling, prepare the grill so that one side is very hot and one side cool. (For a gas grill, you will need two adjacent burners, one turned to high and one turned to low.)

Lightly flour a countertop, unwrap pizza dough, and divide into two or more pieces, depending on how large you want each flatbread. Flatten slightly with your hand, then cover with a clean dishtowel. Rest dough for 10 minutes.

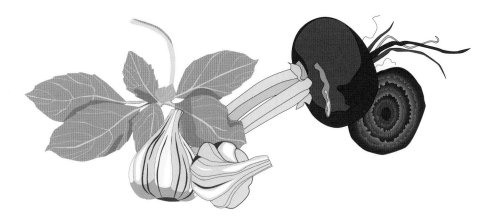

Wash beet greens and dry them well. Remove stems and discard. Chop leaves roughly. Heat 1 tablespoon olive oil in a skillet over medium heat. Add chopped greens, garlic, and 1/2 teaspoon salt. Cook, stirring occasionally, until tender, about 5 minutes. Like most greens, these will cook down substantially. If you like, increase the volume by including some chopped spinach or chard or other green in the pan. Add cooked greens to bowl with sliced beets.

Have at hand a small dish of extra virgin olive oil plus a pastry brush, the prepared beets and greens, crumbled cheese, any additional toppings, and the herbs.

Roll each dough ball into a rough oval or circle 1/4- to 1/2-inch thick. If you find the dough begins to resist rolling, stop working and let it rest 5 minutes to relax the gluten. Then resume shaping.

Baking the flatbread
Place a dough circle on an oiled baking sheet. Brush the dough with olive oil and place baking sheet on top of the preheated pizza stone or hot sheet pan already in the oven. Bake 5 to 8 minutes, depending on the thickness of the dough. It should look dry and start to take on a little color. Remove from oven and top with half the beets, half the greens, half the cheese, and half of any additional toppings. Drizzle with olive oil. Return to oven and bake another 8 to 12 minutes, until crust is brown in spots and cheese has softened. Remove from oven and sprinkle half the fresh herbs on top. Repeat process with remaining flatbread. (If you are making more than two, remember to divide your toppings accordingly.)

Grilling the flatbread
Brush the top of one of the dough circles with olive oil. Place on hot side of the grill, oiled side down, and grill just 1 or 2 minutes, until you can smell the dough charring. While it is grilling, brush the face-up side with olive oil. Flip bread over to the cooler side of grill and brush this side with olive oil. Place a share of the toppings on this flatbread, leaving 3/4-inch around the edges free of ingredients. Use tongs to slide the flatbread back to the hot side of the grill and cook another minute. Remove from grill with a spatula and tongs and sprinkle herbs on top. Repeat with remaining flatbreads, covering grill to bring it back up to temperature before starting the next.

BORSCHT Borscht is one of those traditional foods with a million variants. In the United States we usually know it as a bowl of cold beet soup—a dish for those true fans of beets' earthy flavor. There are so many different ways of making borscht that almost anyone who likes beets can find a variety that suits them. You can serve it hot or cold, with or without meat. You can add onion or garlic, or you can make it milder with the addition of potatoes. Borscht can resemble a mixed vegetable soup, with plenty of tomatoes and cabbage. When my friend Mary sent me a copy of *Canal House Cooking*, I knew I had found the borscht recipe for me. It uses roasted beets, a little onion, bread crumbs, mustard, lots of vinegar, and sour cream. Serve it with chopped hard-boiled egg and rye bread, and now you're talking.

Blueberry Corn Muffins

When I was growing up, our wonderful, retired next-door neighbor, known fondly as Uncle Bill, would make dozens of homemade blueberry muffins that he shared with everyone. Sadly, no one thought to get his recipe before he died. Since then I've never eaten a blueberry muffin I enjoyed quite as much. I now make mine with a corn muffin base. That way, I'm not trying to duplicate Uncle Bill's version, which is, at least in my memory, an untouchable gold standard.

MAKES **12** MUFFINS

8 Tbsp butter

1 3/4 cups flour

1 1/2 cups cornmeal

1 1/2 tsp baking powder

1 tsp baking soda

1/2 tsp salt

2 eggs

1/3 cup sugar

1/3 cup sour cream

3/4 cup buttermilk

2 cups blueberries

Preheat oven to 375 degrees.

Melt butter and remove from heat.

In a large bowl, whisk together flour, cornmeal, baking powder, baking soda, and salt.

In a large measuring cup or a bowl with a spout, whisk eggs and sugar together until thickened. Add sour cream and buttermilk and whisk thoroughly. Finally, whisk in melted butter. Pour this mixture over the dry ingredients, and fold together gently with a rubber spatula. Do not stir briskly, but combine just enough so that only a few streaks of flour are left showing. Gently fold in blueberries.

Line a muffin tin with paper liners. Scoop batter into each section and bake about 24 minutes, until slightly brown on top and a toothpick inserted in the middle of a muffin emerges cleanly. Cool 5 minutes, then turn out of pan to finish cooling. Eat when still warm, or reheat later wrapped in tin foil.

Blueberries

Blueberries may not be the juiciest fruit, and some years their flavor can be, well, subtle. But they have so many positives. Not only are they packed with antioxidants, but they are also sweet, they hold their shape, they keep well, and they appear to be the only naturally occurring blue food. (I remind my children there is no such thing as a "blue raspberry," no matter what any sports-drink company wants them to believe.) In New England you can find both highbush and lowbush blueberries. Both can be found in the wild, but only highbush blueberries are cultivated. The highbush berries are larger, while the lowbush ones are harder to find and are much smaller. Some people swear by one variety over another, but in my opinion, it varies by year. Some years the cultivated blueberries seem very flavorful, and other years the wild ones are far superior.

Blueberry Soup

Scandinavians are known for two types of fruit soup: one made with simmered dried fruit served warm, and one made with berries (sometimes gooseberries, which we don't often see in the United States) thickened with cornstarch and served chilled. This latter soup is tasty enough to serve the leftovers for breakfast, with yogurt, granola, and maybe some honey.

SERVES **4** TO **6**

6 cups blueberries

3 Tbsp lemon juice

1 tsp lemon zest

1 stick cinnamon

3 Tbsp sugar or honey

1/4 tsp salt

1 to 2 Tbsp cornstarch mixed with 2 Tbsp water

1/2 tsp vanilla

1 cup plain Greek yogurt

unsweetened heavy cream, whipped or not, or more yogurt for serving

Combine blueberries, lemon juice, lemon zest, cinnamon stick, sugar, salt, and 1 1/2 cups water in a medium saucepan. Bring to a boil over medium heat, then reduce heat to low and simmer gently for about 5 minutes, stirring often, until berries are completely tender. Whisk in cornstarch mixture and continue heating a few more minutes, until soup thickens slightly.

*(**Note:** The amount of cornstarch you use will determine the thickness. I like to use about 1 1/2 tablespoons, but some like their soup thinner. Keep in mind that the soup will set up more when chilled.)*

Remove from heat and stir in vanilla. Let soup cool for 15 minutes. Remove cinnamon stick.

If you choose, puree part or all of the soup to make it smooth (I don't usually bother). Whisk in yogurt, and chill.

Serve soup topped with a splash of cream or a dollop of whipped cream (traditional) or more yogurt.

Blueberry Bundt Cake

When you're not up to rolling out piecrust, or if you want something a bit easier to transport, this is a great way to serve blueberries to visitors seeking a berry-filled New England experience. A slice of this cake with loads of blueberries peeking out is irresistible to any dessert eater.

SERVES **8** TO **12**

2 3/4 cups flour

1 Tbsp corn or potato starch

2 tsp baking powder

16 Tbsp butter, at room temperature

2 cups sugar

1 tsp salt

1 tsp lemon zest

3 eggs

2 egg yolks

1 Tbsp vanilla

3/4 cup sour cream

3 cups blueberries

Preheat oven to 350 degrees. Grease a Bundt pan very well.

Whisk together flour, cornstarch, and baking powder in a small bowl.

In a mixing bowl, cream butter, sugar, salt, and lemon zest on low speed, with the paddle attachment, for 3 to 5 minutes, until very fluffy. Scrape down bowl. Increase speed to medium and add eggs one at a time, combining well after each. Add egg yolks in same manner. Scrape down bowl.

On low speed, add a third of the flour mixture. When almost completely incorporated, add vanilla and half of sour cream and mix on low until only a few streaks of sour cream remain visible. Repeat. Add final third of flour mixture, mixing until nearly incorporated. Stop mixer and scrape bowl thoroughly. Turn speed to medium-high and beat for 15 seconds, until batter is smooth. Fold blueberries into batter.

Scrape the batter into prepared pan and smooth top. Bake for 10 minutes, then lower heat to 325 degrees and bake for additional 45 minutes. Check for doneness (a toothpick should emerge cleanly). Let cool at least 10 minutes before turning out of pan.

Summer Chard Pasta

My father grew chard in his vegetable garden when I was a kid, but it must have been a vegetable I avoided, because I have no memory of eating it. The first time I remember eating chard was when I helped a friend pick some out of her yard—not garden, yard—where it was growing like a weed. She sautéed it in garlic and olive oil. I couldn't understand why I had missed this vegetable for so many years.

SERVES 4

1 large bunch chard, washed

3 Tbsp extra virgin olive oil, divided

salt

4 cloves garlic, minced or pressed

1 cup walnuts

1/2 cup grated Parmesan cheese, plus extra for serving

1 1/4 cups fresh ricotta

12 oz spaghetti or fusilli

1/2 cup cherry tomatoes, halved

1/2 to 1 cup fresh basil, chopped

Trim the bottoms off the chard stems. Separate the stems from the ribs and slice the stems 1/2-inch thick. Roughly chop the chard leaves.

In a large skillet, heat 2 tablespoons olive oil over medium-high heat. Add the chard stems and 1/2 teaspoon salt and cook for 4 minutes. Add chard leaves and garlic and stir well. Cook an additional 4 or 5 minutes, until chard leaves are wilted and ribs are cooked through. Remove from heat.

Put walnuts and remaining tablespoon of olive oil in a food processor and blend until finely chopped. Stop short of making a paste. You can also chop the walnuts finely by hand and add the olive oil later. Add nuts to the skillet with chard, which should still be warm but off the heat. Add Parmesan and ricotta to skillet as well, along with a ladleful of the cooking water from the pasta. Mix, allowing the ricotta and Parmesan to melt a bit.

Meanwhile, cook the spaghetti in salted water until al dente. Reserve 1 cup of cooking water from the pasta pot. Drain pasta and add to skillet with chard, cherry tomatoes, and basil, mixing well. If sauce seems dry, add more pasta water. When ready, turn into a serving bowl. Serve with additional grated cheese.

Chard

Chard is a mild, nutritious green found all over New England. It has a concentration of oxalic acid in its leaves. This is the stuff that can give your teeth that weird feeling, which some people call "hairy teeth" or "grit." (Spinach has it, too.) To reduce or eliminate this sensation, add another acid, like lemon juice or vinegar. Any type of chard—green, red, or rainbow—works in these recipes. The flavor differences are minimal.

Chard and Egg Pie

Because the eggs remain intact, this dish is really nice when made as several small pies. It makes a great brunch dish or light summer supper. Each small pie serves two people, if they will happily share the single egg, and if there are a few other things to nibble on as well. You can also make a large pie and serve it in slices.

MAKES **3** 4-INCH PIES OR **1** 9-INCH PIE

1 double-crust piecrust,
store-bought, or use recipe for
Cheddar Piecrust

1 large bunch chard

1 Tbsp olive oil

1/2 tsp salt (or more, to taste)

1/2 tsp pepper (or more, to taste)

4 Tbsp cream cheese

2 Tbsp minced fresh basil
or fresh oregano

3 Tbsp bread crumbs

2 Tbsp Parmesan cheese

3 eggs for small pies, 6 for
large pie

for the Cheddar Piecrust
1 1/4 cups flour

1/4 tsp salt

1/8 tsp baking powder

2 oz of cheddar cheese, cut into
1/2-inch cubes to make 1/2 cup

7 Tbsp cold butter, cut into
1/2-inch cubes

1/4 cup cold water

2 tsp cider vinegar

If making small pies, roll the crust into a large rectangle a little less than 1/4-inch thick. Cut out three 7-inch circles of dough. Line three 4-inch pie tins with dough circles. Allow excess crust to hang over sides (do not trim). Place lined tins into refrigerator to keep cold. Re-roll scraps as necessary and cut out three 6-inch circles to serve as tops. Stack them flat, separated by waxed paper, and place in refrigerator.

If making one large pie, divide the crust dough in half and roll out two 11-inch circles, each 1/4-inch thick. Press one into the bottom of a regular pie dish and place the other on a plate lined with waxed paper. Chill until ready to use.

Trim the bottoms from the stems of the chard and discard. Separate the stems from the leaves and cut stems into 1/4-inch-wide pieces. Roughly chop the leaves. Heat olive oil in a medium skillet over medium heat. Add stems and cook 3 minutes. Add leaves, 1/2 teaspoon salt, and 1/2 teaspoon pepper. Sauté until wilted, about 5 minutes. Stir in cream cheese, remove from heat, and cool mixture in pan.

Once cooled, use a slotted spoon to transfer chard mixture to a medium bowl, leaving excess liquid behind. Adjust seasonings to taste. You may want to be generous with the salt and pepper, as the eggs will have no seasoning. Stir in basil, bread crumbs, and Parmesan cheese.

Remove pie pans from refrigerator. For the little pies, spoon some chard filling into each pie plate, covering the bottom crust. Crack an egg on top of the chard in each pan and gently cover each egg with additional chard, using all the filling. Try to avoid breaking the yolk. Drape top crusts over each pie and pinch top and bottom crusts together firmly. Trim any excess dough. Cut a 2-inch slit in the top crust of each pie. Replace pies in refrigerator to chill again. Follow similar steps for the large pie, but make six small wells in the bottom layer of chard and crack the eggs into those wells. Top gently with remaining chard, drape top crust over to fit, and pinch with bottom crust to seal. Cut three vent slits in the top crust and return to refrigerator.

Preheat oven to 425 degrees. Place a rimmed baking sheet in the oven to heat. When oven comes to temperature, place pie tins on preheated sheet and bake for 30 minutes, until crust is browned and steam is emerging from the vent in the crust. Cool 5 minutes before serving.

Cheddar Piecrust

Place flour, salt, and baking powder in a food processor. Add cubed cheese and pulse five times, just until coarse. Add butter and pulse six more times. Add water and vinegar and pulse five or six times, until just combined. Turn out of processor and fold gently a few times, until dough just comes together. Gather together in a ball, wrap in plastic wrap, and chill for 20 minutes before rolling out.

Corn Pudding

This recipe takes a while to bake, but it's a real treat. The sweeter the corn, the greater the treat. The texture is somewhere between a soufflé and a pudding.

SERVES **6** AS A SIDE DISH

6 ears corn, shucked

2 Tbsp butter, plus more to grease baking dish

3/4 tsp salt, divided

1/4 tsp pepper

1/2 tsp sugar

1 cup cream

1/2 cup milk

4 eggs

1 cup grated Monterey Jack cheese

2 Tbsp minced basil, chives, or other fresh herb

Preheat the oven to 350 degrees, and bring 2 quarts of water to a boil. (When it boils, turn off the heat but have it ready to quickly bring to a boil again.) Butter a deep 2-quart casserole dish very well.

Cut the kernels off four of the corn cobs. You should have about 2 1/2 cups' worth. Melt butter in a medium saucepan and add cut corn kernels, 1/2 teaspoon salt, and pepper. Cook for about 5 minutes, stirring occasionally, until kernels just start taking on some color. Add sugar and cream. Cook an additional 3 or 4 minutes, again stirring occasionally, until somewhat thickened. Remove from heat.

Meanwhile, cut kernels off remaining two corn cobs. Place them in a blender with milk, eggs, and 1/4 teaspoon salt. Blend until smooth, 1 to 2 minutes. Pour puree into prepared casserole dish.

Gently stir in whole corn kernels, then top with grated cheese and minced herbs. Place the dish in a roasting pan. Place in oven and fill roasting pan with the boiling water until the water reaches halfway up the casserole sides. Lower heat to 325 degrees and bake 50 to 60 minutes, until pudding has set up but is still wiggly. Test doneness by making a small cut with a knife and peeking at the interior. It should not be runny. Let rest a few minutes before serving.

Corn

Corn on the cob needs nothing more than a short boiling, grilling, or steaming; add butter and salt to make a satisfying dish. As soon as an ear of corn is picked, it gets starchier and less sweet, which is why farmer's market corn is so good. Try to get the corn to your plate as quickly as possible, and keep it cold until ready to cook. At a certain point in the season, my family starts rolling their eyes when I serve up another batch of corn on the cob. That's when I break out one of these recipes.

Tomato Corn Chowder

Once upon a time, chowder was a soup thickened with ship biscuits. Ship biscuits are about as appetizing as they sound, so people generally use other methods these days. In July you should be able to get ripe cherry tomatoes at your farmer's market. They work very well in this recipe. A nice garnish for this soup is chopped zucchini, lightly browned in some olive oil.

SERVES 4

2 pints cherry tomatoes, divided

1/2 tsp salt, divided

4 or 5 ears corn, shucked

3 Tbsp butter

2 shallots, chopped small

1/4 tsp sugar

2 Tbsp flour

3 cups water

1/2 cup heavy cream

pepper

2 Tbsp minced basil or chives

Take 1 cup (1/2 pint) of the tomatoes, cut them in half, and put in a small bowl. Sprinkle with 1/4 teaspoon salt and set aside.

Cut the kernels off the corn cobs. You'll need at least 2 cups' worth. Save the cobs. Set aside 1 cup of kernels.

Melt butter in a medium saucepan over medium heat. Add shallots, sugar, and 1/4 teaspoon salt. Sauté for 3 minutes, until softened. Increase heat to medium-high. Add remaining cup of corn kernels and the remaining 1 1/2 pints of whole cherry tomatoes. Stir well. Cook for about 8 minutes, until tomatoes begin to burst. Add flour and cook for 1 minute, stirring constantly. Gradually pour in water, stirring constantly, and bring to a boil. Reduce to a simmer. Add a few corn cobs to the pot (you may have to break them in half to make them fit), cover, and simmer for 10 minutes, stirring periodically. Remove pot from heat. Discard corn cobs.

Working in batches, puree soup in a blender until smooth. Return to a saucepan over low heat. Stir in the halved tomatoes with any liquid they have exuded, and the reserved uncooked cup of corn kernels. Add cream and heat through. Adjust for salt and pepper. Sprinkle minced basil or chives on top of each serving.

Spinach and Corn Frittata

If you have a sweet red pepper, chop and sauté it along with the onion. It will make this omelet-like dish even more colorful. The size of your skillet will determine exact cooking times. The cooking times below are for a 10-inch skillet. If yours is larger, reduce the time on the stove, and if smaller, increase it. A well-seasoned cast-iron skillet works well here.

SERVES **4** AS A SMALL MAIN COURSE

3 ears corn, shucked

3 Tbsp olive oil, divided

1 bunch spinach, washed and stemmed

1 tsp smoked paprika

1 tsp salt, divided

1/2 small onion, diced

8 eggs

1/2 tsp pepper

4 Tbsp sour cream

2 Tbsp grated Parmesan cheese

2 garlic cloves, minced or pressed

Cut the kernels off the corn cobs. Heat 2 tablespoons olive oil in a large, ovenproof skillet over medium-high heat. Add the corn kernels and cook for 5 minutes, stirring regularly, until they are dry and beginning to brown. Reduce heat to medium. Add spinach, paprika, and 1/2 teaspoon salt and cook another minute or two, stirring often, until spinach is wilted. Remove pan from heat. Using a slotted spoon, remove corn and spinach from skillet. Dispose of any liquid left in skillet.

Return skillet to medium heat and add remaining tablespoon oil. Add onions and 1/4 teaspoon salt. Sauté, stirring occasionally, for 5 minutes, until onion has softened. While onion is cooking, whisk eggs, 1/4 teaspoon salt, pepper, sour cream, and Parmesan in a large measuring cup. Whisk well, so that yolks and whites are fully combined. Preheat broiler to low.

When onions are soft, add garlic and cook, stirring constantly, for 15 seconds. Reduce heat to medium-low and pour in egg mixture. Distribute spinach and corn mixture on top of the eggs. Place a cover over the skillet and cook undisturbed for 6 to 8 minutes. The frittata will start to look dry on the edges; the top will remain wet. It may bubble up, which is fine. Remove cover and place skillet under broiler for 1 to 3 minutes, until browned on top and fully cooked, but not dry. Loosen sides of frittata with a thin spatula and turn upside down onto a serving plate, or remove slices from the pan and serve plated. In either case, you want to remove the frittata from the hot pan to prevent it from continuing to cook and becoming rubbery.

Grilled Shrimp and Corn with Cherry Salsa

When grilling shrimp, sadly, you can't use Maine shrimp; they are just too small and delicate. Try to find shrimp from the Gulf of Mexico. Avoid farmed shrimp from Southeast Asia, as the farming conditions are pretty grim. This recipe calls for a lot of limes—not grown locally, but very nice to eat in the summer.

SERVES **4**

2 cups pitted sour cherries

2 Tbsp honey, divided

1 Tbsp balsamic vinegar

5 Tbsp lime juice, divided

3 1/4 tsp lime zest, divided

2 Tbsp finely chopped sweet onion (or other onion if you don't have sweet)

4 tsp minced garlic, divided

1 Tbsp minced jalapeño or other hot pepper (vary amount to your desired spiciness)

1/4 cup chopped cilantro

1 1/4 tsp salt, divided

1 Tbsp soy sauce

3 Tbsp olive oil

1/4 tsp pepper

1 1/2 lbs large shrimp, peeled and deveined

4 ears corn, shucked

2 Tbsp butter

1/2 tsp smoked paprika

lime wedges, for serving

Coarsely chop the cherries for the salsa. Put in a small bowl and add 1 tablespoon honey, vinegar, 1 tablespoon lime juice, 1/4 teaspoon lime zest, onion, 1 teaspoon minced garlic, jalapeño, cilantro, and 1/2 teaspoon salt. Stir to combine. Let sit at least 45 minutes to combine flavors.

Put 2 teaspoons lime zest, remaining 4 tablespoons lime juice, soy sauce, olive oil, remaining 3 teaspoons minced garlic, remaining tablespoon honey, pepper, and 1/4 teaspoon salt in a large bowl and whisk to combine. Add shrimp and toss to coat. Marinate, refrigerated, for 30 to 60 minutes. Stir once during that time to ensure all pieces stay coated. Remove shrimp from bowl, saving marinade. Thread shrimp onto metal skewers, or wood skewers that have soaked in water, and set on a tray. Pour marinade over shrimp and set aside at room temperature.

Preheat grill to medium-hot. While grill is heating, melt butter with last remaining teaspoon lime zest, 1/2 teaspoon salt, and paprika. Brush the corn with the melted butter mixture. Grill corn for 8 to 10 minutes, letting it blacken in spots, turning regularly. Allow marinade to drip off shrimp before placing skewers on grill. Grill shrimp for 2 to 3 minutes each side. Serve with lime wedges and cherry salsa.

Sour Cherries

Most everyone loves sweet cherries, the crimson Bing and other varieties that are sweet and firm. They are tough to grow in New England except in the southernmost parts, although new varieties are being bred to change that. You'll likely only see sour or pie cherries at the farmer's market. Not everyone likes eating sour cherries out of hand, but they are wonderful for baking and in sauces.

Sour Cherry Shortcake

A shortcake is an extra tender biscuit filled or topped with fruit and whipped cream. Strawberry shortcake is the best known, but there's no need to limit shortcake to one flavor. Juicy sour cherries are great for shortcake too. This is a good recipe to prepare ahead of time. The cherries sit for a while to draw out the juice, and then the juice is reduced. You can also make the biscuit dough ahead of time and refrigerate it, tightly wrapped, until ready to use.

SERVES **6**

For the cherry filling

2 pints sour cherries, pitted

1/3 cup sugar, plus more if needed

1/4 tsp cinnamon

1 Tbsp lemon juice

1 Tbsp brandy

pinch of salt

1/2 tsp vanilla

For the shortcake

2 3/4 cups flour

1/4 cup cornmeal

1 1/2 tsp baking powder

1/4 tsp baking soda

1/2 tsp salt

2 Tbsp sugar, plus more
for sprinkling on biscuits

Place cherries in a medium bowl. Add 1/3 cup sugar, cinnamon, lemon juice, brandy, and salt. Stir and let sit for an hour to macerate. Put a strainer over a saucepan and pour cherries through the strainer. Return cherries to the bowl.

Simmer cherry liquid over medium heat until it is reduced by at least half and somewhat syrupy. The exact time will depend on how much liquid the cherries have exuded, but count on at least 10 minutes. Taste liquid for sweetness. Neither the cherries nor the shortcake are particularly sweet, so if desired, add more sugar and stir to dissolve. Return liquid to bowl with cherries. Stir in 1/2 teaspoon vanilla.

Preheat oven to 425 degrees.

Place flour, cornmeal, baking powder, baking soda, salt, and 2 table-spoons sugar in the bowl of a food processor. Pulse to combine. Add butter chunks. Pulse six or eight times, until mixture is mealy. Turn mixture into a medium bowl.

Whisk together buttermilk, cream, and egg in a measuring cup. Pour over flour/butter mixture and stir gently to combine. You want to dampen the flour mixture, but do not overmix or your shortcake will be tough.

8 Tbsp butter, cold, cut into chunks

1/3 cup buttermilk

2/3 cup heavy cream

1 egg

For the whipped cream
1 1/2 cups heavy cream

1 Tbsp sugar

1/2 tsp vanilla

Turn dough out onto lightly floured counter. Flatten the dough to a rough rectangle about 2 inches thick. Cut into 2 1/2-inch rounds with a sharp metal biscuit cutter or cut into squares with a sharp knife. Set close together on a baking sheet lined with parchment paper or a silicone baking mat. (Baking them close together will keep the sides of the biscuits soft.) Pat remaining scraps into another rectangle and cut out as many rounds as possible. Note that the more the dough is handled, the less tender it becomes. Sprinkle the tops of the biscuits with sugar and bake 12 minutes. Lower heat to 350 degrees and bake another 4 to 6 minutes, until biscuits are puffy and golden. Cool slightly, then use the tines of a fork to gently pull each biscuit horizontally into two halves.

Place heavy cream, sugar, and vanilla in a mixing bowl. Whip to soft peaks.

To assemble the dessert, place the bottom half of a shortcake biscuit on a plate. Top with several spoonfuls of cherries with their juice. Add a large dollop of whipped cream and place remaining half of shortcake on top. Drizzle top with more juice, if desired.

green beans

broccoli

bok choy

August

peppers

okr

peppers

tomatoes

okra

August

**FEATURED
INGREDIENTS**

Bell Peppers,
Bok Choy,
Broccoli,
Green Beans,
Okra,
Tomatoes

BITTERSWEET AUGUST is ridiculously bountiful. It's the month we picture in our heads when we think "farmer's market." Every stall is piled high with vegetables and fruits of all shapes and colors, suggesting so many delicious dishes.

Luscious and bright, tomatoes often take center stage. For good reason these are the most popular homegrown items in the country. A fresh tomato from the garden beats a supermarket version every time. Heirloom varieties have made home cultivation more interesting. Seed catalogs offer hundreds: beefsteak, cherry, plum, slicing, red, yellow, purple, green, striped . . . It's mind-boggling.

Farmer's markets also give us a chance to try these new varieties. Whatever you choose, make sure you buy at least one slicing tomato. One of the great pleasures of summer is a simple sandwich made from a fresh homegrown or farmer's market tomato. My father and I used to enjoy these with the Early Girls he picked every year from his garden. Toast a slice of good bread and spread with your favorite mayonnaise. Top with thick slices of tomato, making sure no bread peeks out. Salt liberally. There's nothing better.

Grilled Peppers with Goat Cheese

My friend Margaret Hathaway, chef and farmer, keeps goats and always has fresh goat cheese on hand. This recipe shows how she pairs it with green peppers. (Note: If you don't have lemon thyme, simply use regular thyme and sprinkle with a small amount of grated lemon zest.)

SERVES **6** AS A SIDE DISH

6 medium, or 12 small, green peppers

2 tablespoons extra virgin olive oil, divided

1/3 cup fresh goat cheese

12 sprigs fresh lemon thyme

1 Tbsp balsamic vinegar (optional)

coarse sea salt

Preheat grill to high. In a large bowl, toss whole peppers with 1 tablespoon olive oil, to coat. Grill over high heat until skin blisters and begins to blacken, and flesh is soft. Alternatively, place peppers under a broiler, turning every minute or so, again until skin blisters.

Slice peppers in half vertically. Remove seeds. Place pepper halves on a large serving platter with cut side up. Crumble goat cheese and divide it evenly among peppers. Drizzle remaining olive oil over the cheese. Arrange sprigs of lemon thyme on the cheese, then drizzle with optional balsamic vinegar and a sprinkle of coarse sea salt. Peppers may be served on their own, with crackers, or with rounds of baguette.

Bell Peppers

There are many ways to enjoy sweet red bell peppers. Cut them up raw, and they're the best part of salads. Ever notice how the red peppers on party veggie platters usually disappear first? It's green peppers—not sweet at all—that are trickier. In Louisiana, celery, onion, and green pepper form the trinity at the base of many gumbos and sauces. The region's cooking is beloved far and wide, so clearly they're on to something.

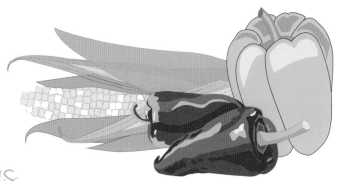

Bell Pepper Rajas

Rajas con crema is a Mexican dish made from strips of peppers (rajas means "strips"), but it's usually made from hot peppers, particularly poblanos. Rajas make a great filling for soft tacos. It's also a nice topping for rice or for grilled chicken or steak. Using bell peppers (of any color) is a fine substitute for the hot peppers. This recipe uses a couple of poblanos to keep things interesting, but you can use only bell peppers if you like to keep things on the mild side. If you don't have a grill to char the peppers, you can either use the burners on a gas stove, or use the broiler.

SERVES **4** AS A SIDE DISH OR TOPPING

4 whole bell peppers

2 whole green poblano peppers

2 Tbsp butter

1 large onion, sliced 1/4-inch thick

1/2 tsp salt

1 cup fresh corn kernels

1/3 cup sour cream

2 Tbsp cream

1/4 cup shredded Monterey Jack cheese

Char the peppers on a hot grill, using tongs to turn them, until the entire skin is blackened. Place peppers on a plate and insert the plate into a large, heavy-duty, resealable plastic bag. Close bag and let the peppers sit for 15 to 25 minutes. The bag will get very steamy. When peppers are soft, remove them from the bag and let them cool a few minutes. Then peel off all the charred skin and discard the skin, stems, seeds, and all liquid from the peppers.

Cut peppers into strips 1/2-inch wide. Be careful not to touch your eyes when working with the poblanos. These peppers can vary a lot in their level of spiciness; usually they are not hot, but every now and then they can pack a punch.

Heat butter in a large skillet over medium heat. Add onion and salt and cook, stirring occasionally, until completely softened and beginning to brown, about 15 minutes. Add corn and cook a few minutes to soften. Add roasted pepper strips and cook for 5 minutes, heating through. Turn heat to low. Add sour cream and cream and stir to combine. Cook a few minutes to heat. Add cheese and stir constantly until cheese has melted. Don't let the dish boil.

Use rajas to build your tacos or top your rice or meat. Keep warm over low heat. If you have to reheat the rajas, do so gently.

Burgers with Potato and Pepper Salad and Bok Choy Slaw

Everything but the burgers can be made ahead of time, which makes this meal convenient if you want to spend the day elsewhere, like at the beach. You may be lucky and find grass-fed beef at the farmer's market. I've read a lot about how important it is to treat grass-fed beef differently, but we've always enjoyed it cooked the same as any beef. It does seem to have more flavor than corn-fed.

SERVES 6

For potato and pepper salad

8 to 10 small to medium potatoes (about 2 lbs), peeled if peels are thick, cut into 2-inch chunks

4 Tbsp rice vinegar, divided

3 Tbsp mayonnaise

3 Tbsp sour cream

1 to 2 Tbsp mustard, whole-grain or Dijon

2 Tbsp capers plus 1 Tbsp brine

3/4 tsp celery seed

salt and pepper

1 to 2 bell peppers of any color, seeded and chopped into 1-inch pieces

1/2 cucumber, peeled if peel is thick, seeded or not, cut into 1/4-inch-thick half-moons

1/2 cup chopped Kalamata olives

2 whole scallions, thinly sliced

1/4 cup minced parsley, cilantro, or basil

Potato and pepper salad

Place potatoes in a medium saucepan and add water to cover by an inch. Salt water generously. Bring to a boil over high heat. Reduce heat to medium and boil until potatoes are tender, 12 to 15 minutes, depending on the size of the potatoes. To test, insert a paring knife into a potato. It should pass through to the center with minimal resistance. Drain potatoes in a colander. Return to cooking pot (not on hot burner) and gently shake for a minute, to allow any moisture clinging to the potatoes to evaporate. Put potatoes in a large serving bowl and pour over them 2 tablespoons of rice vinegar. Stir gently and let sit while preparing remainder of salad.

In a small bowl, whisk together remaining 2 tablespoons rice vinegar, mayonnaise, sour cream, mustard, capers and caper brine, celery seed, 1/2 teaspoon salt, and 1/2 teaspoon pepper.

Pour dressing over potatoes and fold a few times. Add peppers, cucumber, olives, and scallions. Fold until vegetables are well mixed. Adjust seasonings to taste. Sprinkle parsley or other herbs over top. Chill until ready to serve.

Bok Choy

Bok choy is a staple in many Asian cuisines, used in everything from kimchi to dumplings. The cabbage grows well in cool climates, and has recently become popular at farmer's markets in New England. Bok choy is loved for its mild, somewhat sweet taste and signature crunch. It's great in soups and stir-fried dishes. It might look like it's short on flavor and nutritional value, but in fact bok choy is high in vitamin C.

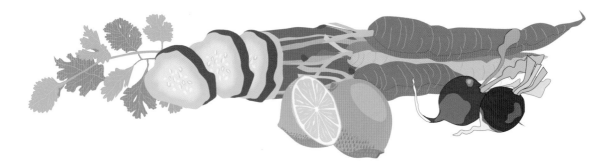

For bok choy slaw

1 head bok choy, end trimmed, thinly sliced

2 or 3 carrots, shredded

6 to 8 radishes, sliced thinly

1/4 cup chopped cilantro or parsley

1/4 cup chopped basil

3/4 tsp salt

2 tsp canola oil

2 Tbsp rice vinegar

1 Tbsp lime juice

1 Tbsp Asian fish sauce

1 clove garlic, minced

1/2 tsp brown sugar

1/2 tsp dry mustard

1/4 tsp red pepper flakes

For burgers

2 lbs ground beef

salt and pepper

6 hamburger buns

Bok choy slaw

Put the bok choy, carrots, radishes, and chopped herbs in a large serving bowl. Toss with salt. In a small bowl, whisk together canola oil, rice vinegar, lime juice, fish sauce, garlic, brown sugar, dry mustard, and red pepper flakes. Pour over vegetables and stir well to combine. This may not seem like enough dressing, but let the slaw sit while preparing hamburgers, and then stir again, incorporating any accumulated liquid. The slaw will now be fully dressed.

Burgers

Preheat the grill with one side very hot, and the other side very low. Form the beef into six patties about 1 inch high, making a slight depression in the center of each patty. Season burgers with salt and pepper on both sides. Place on hot side of grill and flatten slightly with spatula. Grill for 1 minute on each side. Move to cool side of the grill and grill 2 to 4 minutes per side, depending on how done you want your burgers. Grills can differ, but 2 minutes per side on a cool grill gives us medium-rare burgers. While burgers are in their final minutes of grilling, toast the hamburger buns for a minute or so on the hot side.

Place burgers on bun bottoms with tops adjacent (to allow diner to assemble any desired toppings on the burger), and serve slaw and potato salad on the side.

Rice Noodles with Roasted Bok Choy and Tofu

Baby bok choy, if you can get it, roasts very quickly. Larger bok choy, used in this recipe, needs a bit longer. In both cases, roasting is a way to get more flavor than the usual steaming or wilting.

SERVES **4**

2 Tbsp olive oil, divided

2 Tbsp toasted sesame oil, divided

6 Tbsp rice vinegar or lemon juice

3 Tbsp soy sauce

2 Tbsp honey

1 Tbsp minced fresh ginger

5 garlic cloves, minced

2 tsp Asian chili sauce
(like sriracha), or to taste

1 1/2 lbs firm or extra-firm tofu,
cut into 1/2-inch-thick slices

2 bunches large bok choy, washed
and bottom end trimmed

8 oz rice noodles

1 bunch scallions, chopped,
green parts only

1/2 cup cilantro, chopped

1 Tbsp lime juice

Preheat the oven to 450 degrees. Line a rimmed baking sheet with foil and spray the foil with baking spray, or oil it lightly.

In a measuring cup or bowl with a spout, whisk together 1 tablespoon olive oil, 1 tablespoon sesame oil, rice vinegar or lemon juice, soy sauce, honey, ginger, garlic, and chili sauce. Place tofu slices on prepared baking sheet and pour half the sauce over the slices. Roast 15 minutes. Remove from oven and flip each slice. Roast an additional 10 to 15 minutes, until tofu is browned.

Cut the stems off the bok choy leaves. Cut all the stems in half lengthwise and place on a sheet pan. Toss with 1 tablespoon olive oil and roast for 20 minutes. Meanwhile, prepare the leaves. Chop them in half horizontally and in half vertically. After stems have roasted 20 minutes, add leaves to the sheet pan and pour remaining sauce over both. Stir well. Return to oven and roast an additional 5 to 10 minutes, stirring once. Leaves should be wilted and slightly browned in places.

While the bok choy is roasting, prepare the rice noodles. Place them in a large bowl and cover with boiling water. Stir every couple of minutes to prevent them from sticking. When completely limp, taste the noodles to make sure they are cooked through. Drain in a colander and rinse with cold water. Toss noodles with 1 tablespoon sesame oil to reduce sticking.

When bok choy is done, add noodles to roasting pan and stir well to combine. Transfer noodles with bok choy to a large serving bowl. Add scallions, cilantro, and lime juice. Toss. Serve with tofu slices on the side.

Broccoli and Bean Salad

Bean salad is a good change from the usual summer sides of coleslaw and potato salad. And broccoli is a good addition for a change in consistency. Try bringing this salad to a potluck this summer; you may be surprised by how fast it goes.

SERVES **6** AS A SIDE DISH

1 cucumber, peeled if peel is thick, seeded if desired, cut into 1/4-inch-thick half-moons

1 1/4 tsp salt, divided

1 large head broccoli, bottom trimmed

1 lb green beans, trimmed

1/2 medium red onion, sliced thin

3 Tbsp red wine vinegar

1 Tbsp balsamic vinegar

1/2 tsp lemon zest

1 tsp lemon juice

1 garlic clove, minced

2 tsp honey

1/2 tsp pepper

1/3 cup extra virgin olive oil

1 1/2 cups cooked chickpeas

1 1/2 cups cooked red beans (or other cooked beans)

1 cup crumbled feta cheese

1/2 cup chopped fresh basil or chives, or a mixture of fresh herbs

Put cucumber slices into a large salad bowl and toss with 1/2 teaspoon salt. Let sit while preparing remainder of salad.

Cut broccoli stems from florets. Peel stems to remove tough outer layer. Cut stems into 1/4-inch-thick matchsticks no more than 1 inch in length. Cut florets into bite-size pieces no more than 1 inch long. Bring an inch of salted water to boil in a large lidded skillet or saucepan. When boiling, add broccoli pieces and cook, covered, for 90 seconds. Broccoli should be bright green and still have considerable crunch. Drain well in a colander, and spread out on a clean dish towel to cool and dry.

Bring a similar amount of salted water to boil in the same pot. Cook green beans for 90 seconds, until bright green and still crisp. Drain in the colander and run cold water over the beans for 10 seconds or so, to help stop the cooking process. Add to the dish towel with the broccoli to dry out.

Add the sliced onion to the bowl with the cucumber.

To make the dressing, put vinegars, lemon zest, lemon juice, garlic, honey, pepper, and 3/4 teaspoon salt in a small bowl. Gradually whisk in olive oil until emulsified. Add broccoli, green beans, chickpeas, and red beans to salad bowl. Pour dressing over and toss to combine. Add feta cheese and chopped herbs and toss again a few times.

Broccoli

When I was in college, my brother wrote me a letter including the rhyme, "The store was out of broccoli, luckily." He's prone to jokes like that, but I disagree with the sentiment. I love broccoli and always have. Like bok choy, it is a cabbage with a relatively sweet taste and versatility. Serve it steamed, sautéed, or roasted. Just don't overcook it.

Spaghetti with Green Beans, Potatoes, and Basil

One traditional way of eating pesto is with new potatoes and green beans, probably because the two are in season at the same time as a profusion of basil. This is a very satisfying and brightly colored dish, and paired with a tomato salad, it makes a great summer meal.

SERVES **4**

1 or 2 cloves garlic, peeled

salt

3 Tbsp pine nuts or walnuts, toasted or raw

4 cups basil leaves, washed and dried in a salad spinner

1/3 cup grated Parmesan cheese, plus more for serving

3 Tbsp grated pecorino cheese

1/3 cup extra virgin olive oil

1 lb thin green beans, trimmed

12 oz spaghetti or other long pasta with a cooking time of 8 or 9 minutes

5 small new potatoes, cut into 3/4-inch cubes

1 Tbsp butter

To make the pesto, mince the garlic. Sprinkle some coarse salt over the pile of garlic, and mash it several times with the flat of a large knife. Place in the bowl of a food processor. Add pine nuts and pulse a few times. Add basil and pulse a few more times. Scrape down the sides of the bowl. Add cheeses and pulse again to combine. At this point, your basil should still be in pretty large pieces. You are not making it smooth; the final product will have visible pieces of basil leaves. Pour in a tablespoon or so of the olive oil and pulse a few times. Continue this process until all oil has been added and you have an emulsified, finely chopped mixture but not a mushy puree. If you don't have a food processor, use a mortar and pestle to produce your pesto. In that case, add the cheese last; just stir it in.

Bring a large pot of salted water to boil to cook the green beans, pasta, and potatoes. When water is boiling, add the beans only and cook for 3 minutes. Remove from water with a slotted spoon and chop into thirds. Place beans in a large serving bowl and add pesto. Stir to combine.

Bring the pot of water back to the boil and add the potatoes. Cook 3 minutes, allowing water to return to a full boil, and add pasta. Cook until pasta is al dente, at which point the potatoes should be fully tender. While the pasta is cooking, take a small ladleful of the pasta water and add it to the serving bowl with the pesto and beans. Stir gently to loosen the pesto.

Drain the pasta and potatoes and tip them into the serving bowl. Add the butter. Fold gently to combine, coating the pasta and potatoes with pesto. Adjust seasonings and serve with additional grated cheese.

Green Beans

I think green beans are underutilized. They should appear in more salads, as they taste great dressed with a vinaigrette. When roasted, even vegetable agnostics and fussy children will polish them off.

Pan-Fried Okra

Long ago I was struck by farmer / novelist / cookbook author Dori Sanders's statement: "Being a Southerner, I love the okra slime. I could sit there and eat it all day." New Englanders usually try to avoid this aspect of the vegetable. Sanders recommends breading and frying okra when cooking it for Yankees, to reduce the slime. A lot of fried okra recipes call for deep-frying the pieces, or soaking them in buttermilk. You really don't have to fuss with all that. This way is much lighter, quicker, and very tasty. You can make a dipping sauce if you like, or just skip it

SERVES 4 AS A SIDE DISH OR SNACK

5 Tbsp flour

5 Tbsp cornmeal

1/2 tsp turmeric

1 tsp salt, plus more to taste

1/2 tsp pepper

1 lb okra, stemmed, sliced 1/2-inch thick (about 5 cups)

1/4 cup olive oil

Mix the flour, cornmeal, turmeric, 1 teaspoon salt, and pepper in a shallow dish. Dredge the okra slices in the mixture. Heat the olive oil in a large lidded skillet over medium heat. Add the okra and cook, covered, for 10 minutes. Every few minutes, lift lid to stir and check on how okra is doing. It should be starting to brown a little, but if you see anything burning, lower the heat. After 10 minutes, remove the cover. If you have lowered the heat, return it to medium. Cook, stirring often, until pieces are nicely browned, about 5 more minutes. Sprinkle with a pinch or two of coarse salt. Serve right away.

Okra

I never ate okra growing up. In fact, I don't believe I even heard of it until I was in my twenties. Okra has been grown in the United States for centuries; the seeds were probably brought over by African slaves. It is popular all over the South, where cooks use okra's mucilage (not the most appetizing word) as a natural thickener in gumbos. For many native New Englanders, the vegetable still feels novel, and they have yet to appreciate okra's distinct, chewy texture. The recipes here are geared toward those skeptics.

Grilled Okra with Dip

*Grilled okra is a tasty and unusual finger food to offer at New England cookouts. You can serve with any dip you like (the **Green Goddess Dip 2.0** on page 103 goes well with it). You can also toss the okra with more spices if you want. Go crazy.*

SERVES **6** AS A SNACK

2 Tbsp mayonnaise

1/3 cup plain Greek yogurt

1 clove garlic, chopped

1/2 tsp lime zest

1 Tbsp lime juice

1/2 cup chopped chives

8 cherry tomatoes

1 1/2 tsp salt, divided

3/4 tsp pepper, divided

Tabasco sauce to taste

1/4 cup minced basil

3/4 lb (about 4 cups) okra pods (smaller ones are best)

1 Tbsp olive oil

To make the dip, combine mayonnaise, yogurt, garlic, lime zest, lime juice, chives, tomatoes, 1/2 teaspoon salt, 1/4 teaspoon pepper, and a few drops of Tabasco in a blender. Blend until smooth. Pour into a small serving bowl and fold in basil. Refrigerate to blend flavors. This dip is not very thick. If you want it thicker, leave out the tomatoes.

Preheat grill to hot. Trim the stems off the okra pods without cutting off the tops and exposing the seeds. In a large bowl, toss them with 1 teaspoon salt, 1/2 teaspoon pepper, and olive oil. Threading okra pods onto skewers makes grilling a bit easier, but takes more prep time. Poke a metal skewer through the upper part of a half-dozen pods, just below where the stem attaches.

Grill okra over high heat for about 3 or 4 minutes, until char marks show on one side. Rotate skewers or turn pods with tongs and cook on other side for another 3 or 4 minutes. Place on serving platter. Avoid piling pods on top of each other to keep them from getting soggy. The pods don't stay crisp for long, no matter what, but the seeds inside give a nice pop. Serve with dip on the side.

Tomato Pie

My friend Sarah Lougee makes this tomato pie. She also keeps beer on hand, babysits children, and is often available to help people sell cookies at random places and times. She's a good friend, and this is a good pie.

SERVES **6**

3 to 4 big tomatoes, sliced 1/4-inch thick

salt

1/4 cup bread crumbs

1 9-inch piecrust, fully baked (see **Raspberry Yogurt Tart** recipe on page 27 for tart shell directions, or use premade)

1 onion, thinly sliced

1/2 cup basil, thinly sliced

pepper

2/3 cup mayonnaise

1 Tbsp balsamic vinegar

Tabasco or other hot sauce (optional)

2/3 cup shredded cheddar cheese

2/3 cup shredded Monterey Jack cheese

Place tomato slices in a single layer on a very clean dish towel, or several layers of paper towels. Sprinkle salt over and let sit 20 minutes to draw out excess liquid. Blot dry with paper towels.

Preheat oven to 400 degrees.

Scatter the bread crumbs across bottom of the prepared baked piecrust. Place a layer of tomatoes on the bread crumbs, followed by a layer of onion. Sprinkle with basil and give a grinding of pepper. Repeat layers until all ingredients have been used up.

In a medium bowl, mix together the mayonnaise, vinegar, hot sauce, and cheeses. Spread this mixture over the top of the pie, covering completely. Place pie on a baking sheet and bake about 30 minutes, until hot, bubbling, and browned. Let cool 10 minutes before serving.

Tomatoes

August brings such an abundance of tomatoes that more recipes are always welcome. There are only so many tomato sandwiches one can eat, after all.

Tomato Salad

Some years the tomato harvest verges on overwhelming. Those are good years, yes, but they can be stressful if every time you walk into the kitchen you see a giant bowl of tomatoes crying out to be used. When you're not in the mood to be over a hot stove making sauce, try a salad made just of tomatoes with tomato vinaigrette. Add some cubes of toasted leftover bread to make this dish a bit more substantial.

SERVES **6** AS A SIDE SALAD, with extra vinaigrette

2 pints cherry tomatoes, divided

6 large tomatoes, cut into wedges

2 Tbsp extra virgin olive oil, divided

4 tsp balsamic vinegar, divided

1 1/2 tsp salt, divided

1/4 tsp pepper

2 Tbsp chopped basil

additional minced herbs, if desired

Preheat oven to 425 degrees. Place about a dozen cherry tomatoes and eight large tomato wedges on a rimmed sheet pan. Toss with 1 tablespoon olive oil, 2 teaspoons balsamic vinegar, 1/2 teaspoon salt, and pepper. Roast for 15 to 20 minutes, until many of the cherry tomatoes have burst, and the large tomatoes have exuded a lot of liquid. Cool slightly.

Meanwhile, cut each of the remaining cherry tomatoes in half and place in a medium serving bowl. Add the remaining large tomato wedges. Toss with 1 teaspoon salt and let sit while tomatoes roast.

To make the vinaigrette, scrape the roasted tomatoes and their juices into a blender. Place a strainer over the blender. Pour the rested, salted tomatoes over the strainer to collect their juices in the blender as well. Return these drained, unroasted tomatoes to the serving bowl. Toss with basil and any additional minced herbs.

Add 1 tablespoon olive oil and 2 teaspoons balsamic vinegar to blender. Blend until smooth. This makes a relatively thick vinaigrette. It works best to drizzle the dressing over each individual serving of salad.

Save remaining vinaigrette for future salads, or use it as a topping for bruschetta.

ALL THOSE TOMATOES

There are summers when the joy of fresh tomatoes turns slowly to a panic, as the harvest becomes overwhelming. What to do when the mountain of tomatoes on the countertop is growing, no matter how many salads and sandwiches you eat?

Here are a few suggestions.

Gazpacho

Delicious and refreshing, this cold soup has so many variations that you can always find one that fits your available time and vegetable supply. Plus, you don't have to turn on the oven or stove. A couple of my favorite recipes are Yotam Ottolenghi's **Green Gazpacho**, made with green peppers and cucumbers, and *Cook's Illustrated* **Creamy Gazpacho Andaluz**, published in the July 2010 issue, which gets its creaminess from olive oil. Avoid recipes which use canned vegetable juice. They miss the point. You should get plenty of liquid from your fresh vegetables.

Sauce

Fresh tomatoes make delicious sauce. If you don't like canning, just freeze what you make. If you want a thick consistency, say, for spaghetti, you'll have to cook the tomatoes for a while to reduce the liquid, which is a bit sad, because it mutes the fresh taste of summer tomatoes. Using a shorter cooking time will give you a looser but tastier sauce, perfect for homemade pizzas baked at very hot temperatures (when a sauce evaporates a great deal), or for enchiladas or lasagne with no-boil noodles (where a starch is present to absorb some of the liquid).

Drying

You can use a specialized dehydrator to make your own dried tomatoes, and they do come in handy for apples as well. But you can also oven-dry your tomatoes, just by cooking them at a low oven temperature (200 to 250 degrees) for a few hours. You can then store them in your freezer for later use in soups, stews, and sauces.

Chutney

Tomato chutney is a tasty condiment which makes a great addition to summertime sandwiches and breakfasts. Chutney can be cooked on the stovetop or in the oven, with plenty of your favorite seasonings added to the chopped tomatoes. Even without canning, chutney can keep for a month in the refrigerator.

Acknowledgements

FIRST, THIS BOOK WOULD NOT EXIST without the vision and hard work of Melissa Kim, project manager extraordinaire at the wonderful Islandport Press. Thank you for everything. I am deeply in your debt.

The recipes and text would be impossible to follow and ridiculously long without the amazing attention to detail of editor Nancy Heiser. And I would have been a nervous wreck without her tact. Thank you for your patience and for how much you have taught me. Thank you to proofreader and copy editor Melissa Hayes for her stunning attention to detail.

Thank you to all my recipe testers for your cooperation and spirit of adventure: Annie Adamsky, Sarah Buchanan, Sarah, Charlie, and Oliver Compton, Mary Cunningham, Alison Kenway, Amy Lilavois, Nicki Lilavois, Triona O'Connor, Jen Peavey, Derek Pelletier, Rachel Schumacher, Rachel Simons, and Maryann Welsch. Special thanks to Kari-Lise Richer, Margaret Hathaway and Karl Schatz, Emily Brackett and Randy Woods, and Lisa Plimpton and Dave LaBranche (you all know why!!). I am lucky to have friends and relatives with nitpicky, OCD tendencies. Thank you all.

Thank you to Teresa Lagrange. I hope the recipes live up to your beautiful artwork, but that's a tough task indeed. And thanks to designer Karen Hoots, for putting the whole thing together so elegantly.

Thank you to a very patient spouse who washed a lot of dishes and ate a lot of kohlrabi and celeriac. Thank you to Archie and Harry, who ate some kohlrabi and celeriac, learned to love beets, and waited a long time for taco night. Thank you to my mother and the Massachusetts Scandinavian Underground for sharing their secret recipes.

And to my father——thank you for those tomato sandwiches.

Elise Richer

Resources

Farmer's Markets and Community Supported Agriculture

A starting resource for finding a nearby farmer's market or CSA is LocalHarvest (**www.localharvest.org**). It is a national resource and so may not always have the most up-to-date information about local food, but the exhaustive website is a great place to begin.

Each state in New England has at least one umbrella group (sometimes run through the state's Department of Agriculture) which seeks to facilitate the production and consumption of food grown and distributed in the region, including through farmer's markets and CSAs.

BuyCTgrown is a public-private partnership seeking to bring Connecticut farms and their produce closer to the public. At its website, the public can find farmer's markets, CSAs, farms and producers, and events and activities.
buyctgrown.com

The Maine Federation of Farmers' Markets is a volunteer-run nonprofit which gathers and disseminates information on the state's more than 130 farmer's markets.
www.mainefarmersmarkets.org

The Maine Department of Agriculture's "Get real, get Maine" campaign includes an excellent website, which provides a number of ways to search for farms, markets, and CSA programs across the state.
www.getrealmaine.com

The Massachusetts Department of Agriculture has a "MassGrown" website with information about all the state's farmer's markets, CSA farms, local produce, and activities.
www.mass.gov/agr/massgrown/

The New Hampshire Farmer's Market Association is a nonprofit organized to assist farmers in selling their produce locally. Consumers can find lists of farmer's markets and what's in season at the NHFMA website.
www.nhfma.org

The New Hampshire Department of Agriculture, Markets and Food publishes an annual list of CSAs as well as a list of farmer's markets, farms by commodity, and more.
agriculture.nh.gov

The nonprofit Farm Fresh Rhode Island gathers information and incubates agricultural businesses in the Ocean State. Farm Fresh lists farmer's markets and CSAs throughout Rhode Island and southern New England.
www.farmfreshri.org/

The Vermont Agency of Agriculture runs a "Buy Local, Buy Vermont" program listing farmer's markets, CSAs, and production facilities for Christmas trees, textiles, and nurseries.
www.vermontagriculture.com/buylocal/buy/

 CONTINUED

There are a number of state and regional organic farmers' associations which are very active in selling local produce. Many organize events promoting local and sustainable agriculture. The umbrella organization for the region is the Northeast Organic Farming Association. **www.nofa.org**

Connecticut, Massachusetts, New Hampshire, Rhode Island, and Vermont all have organic farming organizations under this umbrella, and their sites are also good resources for finding farms, markets, and CSAs. Maine has its own independent organization, the Maine Organic Farmers and Gardeners Association. Every September, MOFGA organizes the wonderful Common Ground Country Fair in Unity, Maine, which is an excellent venue to learn about the world of local agriculture. **www.mofga.org**

Additional Sources

Slow Food USA is the American arm of an international movement to celebrate and preserve local food customs and products; New England currently has 18 state and local chapters. Each chapter holds events and disseminates information about its activities. **www.slowfoodusa.org**

A private citizen with a great love of local food runs the PickYourOwn website. It's a terrific place to find local pick-your-own farms, plus you can see what's in season in your area. It also offers lots of advice for canning and preserving. A similar website geared toward locating farmer's markets is in the works as well. **www.pickyourown.org**

For information on the availability, sustainability, and cleanliness of local seafood, a good place to start is the Monterey Bay Aquarium's famous Seafood Watch program. **www.montereybayaquarium.org**

The Environmental Protection Agency provides tools for finding local seafood advisories and also provides links to each state's website. The state websites often provide very consumer-friendly advice on the best fish to eat in your region. **www.fishadvisoryonline.epa.gov**

Farmers in California can take advantage of their climate to produce all kinds of crops we can't raise here in New England. Still, Evan Kleiman's weekly Los-Angeles based "Good Food" show, broadcast on KCRW and available as a podcast, is a great resource for farmer's market cooking even for those of us in the Northeast. Each week's show begins with an update on what is available at the Santa Monica farmer's market, and what chefs are doing with the local produce available. The show provides culinary inspiration as well as a ton of information and, to those of us on the puritanical East Coast, outrageous trend-spotting.

Storing Vegetables

Recommended books and websites with information on how to store vegetables:

Grow Cook Eat: A Food Lover's Guide to Vegetable Gardening, including 50 Recipes, Plus Harvesting and Storage Tips by Willi Galloway, photographs by Jim Henkens (Sasquatch Books, 2012). This is an excellent resource for home gardeners and preservers.

Root Cellaring: Natural Cold Storage of Fruits & Vegetables by Mike Bubel, Nancy Bubel (Storey Publishing, 1991).

The Complete Root Cellar Book: Building Plans, Uses and 100 Recipes by Steve Maxwell and Jennifer MacKenzie (Robert Rose, 2010).

The Complete Guide to Your New Root Cellar: How to Build an Underground Root Cellar and Use It for Natural Storage of Fruits and Vegetables by Julie Fryer (Atlantic Publishing Company, 2011).

Many public universities in New England have cooperative extension programs which provide advice on storing local fruits and vegetables.

The University of Maine, for instance, has a Gardening and Horticulture extension which distributes tips on harvesting, storing, and preserving fresh produce.
http://umaine.edu/gardening/master-gardeners/manual/vegetables/

The University of New Hampshire has collected a number of helpful links on harvesting and preserving crops.
http://extension.unh.edu/hcfg/Harvest_Preserv.htm

The University of Rhode Island's Food Safety Education has links to documents that cover a wide range of food storage and preservation topics.
http://web.uri.edu/foodsafety/foodPreservation/

The University of Vermont's "Eating What We Grow" program offers a series of handouts about local produce, including recipes and short tips on selecting good-quality items and how to store them.
http://www.uvm.edu/extension/food/?Page=grow.html

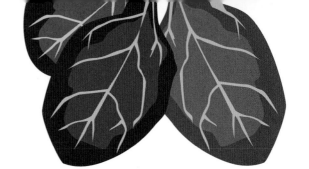

Seasonal Menus

Index

A note on saltiness: *All the recipes assume the use of kosher salt. If you are using table salt, please halve the quantity of salt indicated.*

V *indicates vegan recipe, or easily made vegan (i.e., by leaving out an ingredient, or swapping oil for butter, etc.).*

GF *indicates gluten-free recipe, or easily made gluten-free (i.e., by leaving out one ingredient). Please note that these recipes are gluten-free only if proper care is taken with ingredients such as vinegar, wine, soy sauce, mayonnaise, etc., to ensure that only gluten-free versions are used.*

About the Author

Elise Richer *has worked in several restaurants, run her own baking business, and cooked a lot of family meals. As a teenager in Massachusetts, she worked at a farm stand where she learned how much tastier a Macoun is than a Macintosh. As an adult, she lived and worked in Washington, DC, where she was spoiled by a long growing season and abundant peaches. She moved to Maine in 2003 and has been learning to love cabbage ever since. Elise lives in Portland with Mark, Harry, Archie, Willie, and Smoke.*

About the Illustrator

Teresa Lagrange *is an illustrator/graphic designer who lives in Portland, Maine. She enjoys using bright, bold colors in her digital illustrations, but also creates soft watercolors and drawings. A graduate of University of Maine, she has worked as a designer for the University of Connecticut and the Portland Museum of Art. She has also written and illustrated a children's book,* The Twelve Days of Christmas Island. *When she isn't sketching on any paper she can find, or creating art on the computer, Teresa enjoys being with her family and spending time outdoors. She lives with her husband Jim, children Grace and Jack, two cats, and a dog.*

Notes